PRAISE

THROUGH THE EYES OF LOVE

"Shawn Bolz is a personal favori̇̇ne ... ain to recalibrate the hearts of many that we might accurately represent the heart of God, the heart of Love."

—BILL JOHNSON, SENIOR LEADER, BETHEL CHURCH, REDDING, CALIFORNIA; AUTHOR OF *THE RESTING PLACE*

"Shawn reminds us how we are all called to love people by being the hands and feet of Jesus on this planet. This book will challenge you to not just see others through God's eyes, but to do something about it."

—CHRISTINE CAINE, BESTSELLING AUTHOR; FOUNDER, A21 AND PROPEL WOMEN

"Through the lens of love, we become vessels of love—releasing healing to a hurting world. I recommend this book because I respect Shawn, whom God is working through mightily . . . because he views the world through the eyes of love."

—JOHN BEVERE, MINISTER AND BESTSELLING AUTHOR; COFOUNDER OF MESSENGER INTERNATIONAL

"After reading this book, you will walk away personally impacted by the Father's heart for you and those around you, inspired by the powerful testimonies Shawn shares and more connected to the heart of God!"

—KRIS VALLOTTON, SENIOR ASSOCIATE LEADER, BETHEL CHURCH, REDDING, CALIFORNIA; AUTHOR OF *POVERTY, RICHES, AND WEALTH*

"Let Shawn take you through these powerful real-life stories into the beautiful discovery of the God who loves you. This book has the power to change your life and how you see the supernatural world all around you. Encounter God through the eyes of love!"

—BRIAN SIMMONS, AUTHOR OF *THE SACRED JOURNEY*; LEAD TRANSLATOR OF THE PASSION TRANSLATION

"This book will reveal to you that the prophetic is applicable and functional in literally every area of life. It demonstrates that the world is waiting for you to activate your prophetic gift. Are you ready? Are you ready for this encounter, for this adventure? Let's go—"

—ROBBY DAWKINS, PASTOR, AUTHOR OF *DO WHAT JESUS DID*

"Shawn, thank you! This book is rich, revelatory, and empowering. Thanks for being a voice that represents love himself so well. Thanks for raising the bar!"

—PATRICIA KING, FOUNDER OF PATRICIA KING MINISTRIES; COFOUNDER OF XPMEDIA.COM

"No matter where you may be on this journey, this book will stir a hunger inside of you to step into all God has for you. You cannot read these stories and remain unprovoked by a God who is in pursuit of people to reveal His love to them. Shawn will challenge your paradigms and I am grateful for that."

—BANNING LIEBSCHER, FOUNDER AND PASTOR OF JESUS CULTURE; AUTHOR OF *ROOTED*

"*Through the Eyes of Love* is a core resource for exploring the prophetic and its significance in our everyday lives. There is so much valuable wisdom here."

—CHÉ AHN, SENIOR PASTOR, HROCK CHURCH; PRESIDENT, HARVEST INTERNATIONAL MINISTRY; INTERNATIONAL CHANCELLOR, WAGNER UNIVERSITY

"By using stories and helpful conversations, Shawn illustrates how to hear from heaven's viewpoint and bring Christ's redeeming love, hope, and solutions to people in every situation. I recommend that you read this book from cover to cover; you will be inspired and your faith stirred to impact the world all around you."

—GEORGIAN BANOV, PRESIDENT AND COFOUNDER OF GLOBAL CELEBRATION AND THE GLOBAL CELEBRATION SCHOOL OF SUPERNATURAL MINISTRY

"As human brokenness is materializing on the planet in many different forms, Christ is calling the body to function 'through the Eyes of Love.' I am honored to call Shawn Bolz a friend. Shawn has the character, humility, and revelation to bring this message to humanity."

—Brian "Head" Welch, cofounder of the Grammy Award–winning band Korn; bestselling author of *Save Me from Myself*; costar of *Loud Krazy Love*

"What I most love about Shawn and Cherie is their absolute intention and passion to know by experience the nature of God and to make that both known and attainable for others. This book is a life changer and in some circumstances, a lifesaver."

—Graham Cooke, speaker and author, www.brilliantperspectives.com

"This will become a landmark book that will impact believers to use the gift of prophecy as a tool of evangelism and love. I'm thrilled to endorse it and encourage people to spread the word: prophecy is a gift of hope and compassion."

—Paul Marc Goulet, senior pastor, International Church of Las Vegas

"This penetrating message of loving people is just the message we need to hear in our often hypercritical world. Shawn is real. His transparency is refreshing. Please read all of this book from cover to cover."

—Cindy Jacobs, cofounder, Generals International

"*Through the Eyes of Love* opens up fresh adventures and opportunities for each of us to exhibit love in our vertical walk with the Lord and our horizontal walk with mankind. What the world needs now is love, and Shawn Bolz is paving a way that we can each follow."

—James W. Goll, founder of God Encounters Ministries; author, communications trainer, consultant, and recording artist

"If you want to connect with the heart of God—for yourself and for your world—so that you will live in the fullness of your destiny, look no further. This book will make you laugh and will make you cry and will shape your mind and heart with the beauty of God's affection for humanity. Be prepared to be challenged, inspired, and mobilized."

—JULIAN AND KATIA ADAMS, DIRECTORS OF FREQUENTSEE

"*Through the Eyes of Love* is a beautifully written book connecting God's love for us with our ability to hear Him. The stories and teaching in this book allow us to move into a new dimension of understanding."

—BOB HASSON, COAUTHOR OF *THE BUSINESS OF HONOR*

THROUGH THE EYES OF LVE

ENCOURAGING OTHERS THROUGH PROPHETIC REVELATION

SHAWN BOLZ

EMANATE
BOOKS

© 2019 Shawn Bolz

All rights reserved. No portion of this book may be reproduced, stored in a retrieval system, or transmitted in any form or by any means—electronic, mechanical, photocopy, recording, scanning, or other—except for brief quotations in critical reviews or articles, without the prior written permission of the publisher.

Published in Nashville, Tennessee, by Emanate Books, an imprint of Thomas Nelson. Emanate Books and Thomas Nelson are registered trademarks of HarperCollins Christian Publishing, Inc.

Thomas Nelson titles may be purchased in bulk for educational, business, fund-raising, or sales promotional use. For information, please e-mail SpecialMarkets@ThomasNelson.com.

Unless otherwise noted, Scripture quotations are taken from the Holy Bible, New International Version®, NIV®. Copyright © 1973, 1978, 1984, 2011 by Biblica, Inc.™ Used by permission of Zondervan. All rights reserved worldwide. www.zondervan.com. The "NIV" and "New International Verion" are trademarks registered in the United States Patent and Trademark Office by Biblica, Inc.™

Scripture quotations marked HCSB are taken from the Holman Christian Standard Bible®, copyright © 1999, 2000, 2002, 2003, 2009 by Holman Bible Publishers. Used by permission. HCSB® is a federally registered treademarks of Holman Bible Publishers.

Scripture quotations marked KJV are taken from the King James Version.

Scripture quotations marked THE MESSAGE are taken from The Message. Copyright © by Eugene H. Peterson 1993, 1994, 1995, 1996, 2000, 2001, 2002. Used by permission of Tyndale House Publishers, Inc.

Scripture quotations marked NASB are taken from the New American Standard Bible®, Copyright © 1960, 1962, 1963, 1968, 1971, 1972, 1973, 1975, 1977, 1995 by The Lockman Foundation. Used by permission. (www.Lockman.org)

Scripture quotations marked NKJV are taken from the New King James Version®. © 1982 by Thomas Nelson. Used by permission. All rights reserved.

Any Internet addresses, phone numbers, or company or product information printed in this book are offered as a resource and are not intended in any way to be or to imply an endorsement by Thomas Nelson, nor does Thomas Nelson vouch for the existence, content, or services of these sites, phone numbers, companies, or products beyond the life of this book.

The names of some of the individuals featured throughout this book have been changed to protect their privacy.

ISBN 978-0-7852-2730-4 (eBook)
ISBN 978-0-7852-2729-8 (TP)

Library of Congress Control Number: 2019938071

Printed in the United States of America
19 20 21 22 23 LSC 10 9 8 7 6 5 4 3 2 1

CONTENTS

FOREWORD

"I've released you from your work here."

My dad turned toward my mom as he said, "Jan, you won't believe what the Lord just said to me!"

Her immediate response was, "No, I will, because the Lord just said the same thing to me: He's released us from our work here!"

That was the voice of the Lord in 1973.

So, when it comes to the idea of hearing God's voice, I immediately think of that season in time when my mom and dad first received their marching orders from the Lord, leading to the founding of what we know today as TBN.

Those seven unmistakable words resulted in the world's largest and most watched faith-and-family broadcaster, now reaching more than 175 nations across the earth with inspirational and entertaining programming twenty-four hours a day in fourteen languages and on thirty-two networks around the globe.

But why wouldn't God speak to His children this way?

Jesus Himself declared, "Man shall not live by bread alone but by every word that proceeds out of the mouth of God." Contextually, Jesus spoke this to the Devil during His desert experience while being tempted with "all the kingdoms of this world." But that's how paramount the Word of God is.

Some seem to believe that every word that proceeds out of the mouth of God has already been spoken or written in the canonized scriptures. However, I believe such a mind-set is shortchanging an eternal God who is still calling things into existence today for those who are willing to listen to the still, small voice and follow.

Over the years of following Him, many of us in Christendom have experienced this truth and understand that God's voice is ongoing and both loving and instructive to His children—very much along the lines of Jeremiah 29:11, "I know the plans I have for you, declares the Lord, to prosper you and not to harm you, plans to give you a hope and a future."

Laurie and I experienced this personally when we felt unmistakably called to Hollywood, producing motion pictures by God's grace, one—*The Omega Code*—to become *The Hollywood Reporter*'s number one Independent Film of the Year. But we also heard it just as clearly when we were abruptly called back out of Hollywood to walk away from the company we'd built and rejoin the staff of TBN, having no idea at the time we would one day be leading the ministry.

I truly appreciate Shawn's chapter on "Prophecy in Life Direction" where he aptly says, "Encounters with God help us get in touch with our God-given identity, and our lives naturally change directions as a result. And sometimes when we are simply walking with God through regular seasons of life, we sense that following His plan means making a massive life change."

I'm sure that if you've been walking with God for any length of time, you too have experienced both the "regular seasons of life" and perhaps the upheaval of "massive life change." But one thing is for sure, walking with God and listening to "every word that proceeds out of the mouth of God" in your life is never boring! His ways are higher than ours.

Through the Eyes of Love will forever codify in your heart of hearts the fact that God loves His children enough to be intimately involved in their relationships (starting with Himself), their marriages and families, personal identities, restoration when needed, finances, and their lives' direction.

Enjoy this book. I certainly did.

Matt Crouch

INTRODUCTION

Our mighty God is ever present in our lives. He is not just in a church building or in organized Christian evangelism. He is a God who wants to be involved in the details of our lives and to infiltrate all areas of culture.

God's love is not meant to be esoteric, broad and detached from real life. God's love looks and sounds like something tangible in our world. We can see His love at work in all realms of society today: business, education, government, entertainment, families. It is also present in and has a valuable perspective on everything we struggle with—identity, health, relationships, employment, money, life transitions, the restoration of what is broken.

I'll be addressing these areas of life throughout this book, sharing stories that reveal what God's eyes of love see in these situations and explaining how we, too, can look through His eyes of love.

As Christians we are to be known by God's empowering love living in us, a kind of love that can only come from Him. His love isn't just good ideas and warm fuzzies; it's a love that transforms. When we experience it, we will be able to live our destinies fully. It will cause us to collectively engage all areas of our world, from churches to brothels, to be God's love to them, and to see God transform and restore them.

I wrote this book to boast in what God is doing and to help you and those around you be transformed by hearing this voice of love. You will discover the kind of transformation that can happen when we partner with God—when we see with His eyes, do what He does, and speak what He speaks. His love creates opportunities for us to align ourselves with truth and goodness, to empower us to be who He created us to be. His love will help you and those around you to thrive.

Who knows how God might want to bring new healing, peace, and strength to your heart? Who knows how He might want to use you to reach others through hearing His voice of love?

I want to ignite your faith and invite you to a realm you may never have imagined was available to you. It is more available than what many would guess. I do ask that you suspend your belief system—be open to being activated and charged by these stories. Go on a journey of discovering this voice for yourself. Do what the Jews in Acts 17:11 did: they received the message about God and God's love, and they searched the Scriptures to see if the message was true.

I pray that your eyes will be opened to see God's love in ways that are beyond what you could imagine. Begin, or continue, your journey as you let your faith be jump-started through these stories.

1

CONNECTING WITH
THE FATHER

What would change if you looked at your life with a scale of love weighing every interaction? What if your value system were truly rooted in love, impacting every decision you made? What would change if you looked at others through the eyes of love, or if you spoke God's words of love to the world? To your family? To your identity? These questions are central to the perspective of biblical living.

These questions drive me to do what I do with my life—to seek and live out solutions found only through a connection to love. This book is full of stories about the answers to these questions, and stories about what happens when we look at any situation with God's love and find that everything we thought we knew can transform before our eyes.

When we look through the eyes of God's love, the impossible becomes possible. After all, we know from Scripture that His love removes our sins from us as far as the east is from the west. It restores shattered hearts, sets captives free, breaks bondages, brings hope to the hopeless, creates beauty out of nothing, and brings death back to life! This is the power of love, and these are the possibilities God sees when He looks at us. This can become our own perspective in our daily lives.

Not only does God show us His amazing love, but He also speaks to us. Almost every significant story in the Bible is about God speaking to a person and that person making choices because of his or her relationship with Him. Our whole journey of connection to God is hinged on the fact that He communicates with us. He gave us the Bible, the Word. Jesus promised that the Holy Spirit would come and speak to us, and then the book of Acts takes us on the journey of how that worked for the first Christians. These were prototype experiences, and just like everything else in the Bible, they reveal how our God has a unique personality. As we get to know Him, we can reveal His awesomeness to the world around us. He speaks through men and women who hear His voice and speak what He sees, and He uses them to bring about His heart and His intention to the world today.

When God's voice comes, it doesn't just provide a passive suggestion; His word creates unimaginable opportunities. It creates a way for His plan and design and love to be expressed in the world. It creates an opportunity for His heart to be revealed, a situation to be redeemed, a successful business to be established, a stunning building to be constructed, a parent to be led in raising a family. God cares about everything that has to do with us and wants to empower us to go further than we've imagined. God's heart is not to obliterate ourselves and our culture but to infiltrate every part of us and all areas of culture. He wants to align all of it with His love, which can transform and restore everything He created to the fullness of His original plan and purpose.

Hearing from God allows us to be in touch with this great love and changes our options for how to value and treat the world around us. Hearing from God also enables us to know what is going on in the inner thoughts of our Father God in a close, intimate, and personal way (1 Corinthians 2:6–16). You don't just read about it; you experience the Spirit of God, who is relating His feelings, thoughts, desires, and even plans for how His love is going to build around you.

It is this love that motivates me daily in my pursuit of God. I get to understand the incredible way that love is showing up in people's lives. When you look through love's eyes and see what is in God's heart and imagination, you become powerful. You set yourself up to be backed up with the life force of God—the God who created the world, set it into motion, and made you. His words of love still have the power to shape and impact every situation in our world today.

It is also this love that has motivated me to be part of the transformation of others—to take in foster-care boys and share my life and love with people in terrible situations and war zones.

It is also this love that prompted me to start a church and ministry in Los Angeles, California. To reach successful people, especially those in Hollywood and entertainment industries (many of whom are sometimes hard to love because of their tremendous egos and narcissism) with God's love. To reach people who are homeless, having no resources or positive connections in life, with God's love. No one is too lost for us to love.

Throughout my life I have traveled the world hearing and seeing so many ways God shows His love. Each encounter has filled me with joy and hope and awe at who God is and the lengths He will go to love people who, frankly, I don't always think deserve it. Every month I speak to millions of people about this topic. Every week I spend time looking for what love is seeing and then speak what I see to the people around me. Almost daily I get to watch the power of love transform lives, hearts, and situations around me.

Every time I see what God sees, I get excited. When He shows me His love, and when He speaks love through me, I am like a child at Christmas. Not because it brings me personal significance, but because it builds my intimacy with God, and it brings my heart joy to hear the secrets of people's hearts and see God's love move them. I get to take part in God's work of revealing His nature and love. In that moment I feel the impact of God's masterful care for another person, and I think, at the end of the day, that is the most valuable thing we can give, receive, and be a part of.

This does not have to be some magical, mystical, supernatural moment when angels come and sing. This happens often in regular, everyday life.

TRANSFORMED IN AN EVERYDAY MOMENT

My friend we'll call Christine used to work with a residential program for at-risk youth who were in difficult life situations and living away from home. One day Christine was sitting with a teenager named Michael who had a violent background, and with no warning, he became extremely angry. He began threatening her with physical violence, cursing, and yelling, "I hate you!" He was in a fit of rage.

Christine could have called security guards immediately or tried to overpower Michael and put him in his place. Instead, she was reminded of Jesus, how He asked God to forgive those who were murdering Him while they were in the act of killing him. She thought of love in the flesh, the One who loved even when He was despised by men and women. In that moment she felt God leading her not to call for support from others, that He had a different solution.

"Michael, it's okay if you hate me now, and forever," Christine said. "I'm okay with that. It doesn't change what I think of you. Even if you were to hurt me, I would do what I could to protect myself, but I would still care for you and want the best for you—no matter what you say or do to me."

This was acceptance Michael didn't deserve. Something about this wonderfully kind woman's expression of love made his eyes fill with tears. Then they were streaming down his face. Christine consoled him, and before long he was talking to her about how hard his life had been, about the abuse and pain he had lived through. She loved him simply by listening.

Christine felt love form into a spiritual word for Michael. She prophesied over this very sad, broken young man and shared two words of knowledge God knew about the pain in his life.

He was stunned that he was so known. He didn't feel anyone in his life had ever truly known him, that anyone knew what he had walked through. He thought he was isolated in his pain, but here was Jesus, through Christine, telling him all about himself! Something inside him broke open. Love had come.

It didn't stop there, though. Christine also shared about

who Michael was. God had gifted him in leadership, and he was called to serve as a leader. She said that he was God's good creation, that he was meant for good things, and that God had good things for him to lead others into.

Christine simply listened, prophesied over, and encouraged Michael for about an hour, and he was never the same.

The next day others came to Christine and asked her what she did, because after that one conversation, Michael was completely different to his peers and the staff at the house. He was now creating a culture of acceptance and empowerment for those around him. He was displaying a hopeful and encouraging attitude.

The words Christine spoke to Michael were not her own; she had seen love. She was treating this young man the way God wanted him to be treated. These words of love called Michael into a different frame of being. It created an option of a new identity for him to walk into, one that wasn't there before. Through Christine, the unconditional love of God crashed into a terrible situation and everything that Michael thought he knew changed. From that day on, he remained different.

There was no manual for how to make that happen. But there was love, and connecting with God about how He wanted to show love to Michael, and receiving the specific words he needed to hear at that specific moment. Everything in Michael's life changed because of someone showing God's love and helping Michael see through the eyes of love.

When we see through love's eyes, we can see a person as he or she was created to be. But connecting people to the Father's love is not just about speaking love. To demonstrate His heart fully, love has to listen. If Christine had not listened first, Michael might have never received what she said next.

Sometimes no words need to be said. We can treat people with the value that God has for them instead of how we would treat them without knowing this value. There have been times when I could see that no spiritual word or great encouragement would be enough to reach a person because, given the condition of his or her heart, that person would not be able to receive it. Sometimes it's all about actions. Giving a hug, offering a listening ear, or buying a homeless person a pillow can be the communication of love that prophesies to a person's heart about who he or she is. The words we say and the knowledge we have do not make us great; our acts of great love make us great.

When Jesus heard that there was a man up in a tree named Zacchaeus who the Father wanted Him to spend time with, Jesus took action—even though everyone around Him tried to convince Him that the man wasn't worthy. He went anyway and spent the time. He didn't explain why. That action was enough to communicate full love and acceptance.

The desire to be profound or to qualify everything with words will always lead us the wrong way. In order to reach people with God's love, we must constantly practice childlike faith and follow the Father where He leads.

GOD'S LOVE CREATES NEW POSSIBILITIES

God's love can be quiet and steady, or it can crash into our lives when we least expect it. Either way, it creates opportunities when everything we can see indicates that there is no opportunity left.

Take Moses, for example. He and all of Israel were trapped,

with the Red Sea in front of them and an army chasing them toward the sea from all three sides. But God's love for His people came. His rare and very real love provided a new option, one that no one thought was possible: He parted the Red Sea. This was a miracle, yes, but not just a miracle for fun; it was a miracle to demonstrate the limitless love the Father has for His people.

God did something no one thought was possible with Mary too: the virgin became pregnant with Jesus.

God's love for the world empowered Jesus to demonstrate signs and wonders on the earth.

The Bible is full of stories of God's showing us just how much is possible through His love! And He is still parting the Red Seas in our lives today. God is bringing His love and everything is changing in its wake.

But, you might be thinking, *the world is complex. Sometimes it is hard to know what love is.* I've been there. Is it love to give a homeless person cash if we are afraid they will spend it on drugs that will hurt them? Is it good to love someone who has hurt us and will likely hurt us again? How can we look at a situation and know what love sees?

OUR ULTIMATE GUIDE TO LOVING

First John 4:8 says, "God is love." Jesus is our best example of this. John 1:14 says Jesus is the Word of God "made flesh" (KJV). So, if God is love, and Jesus is the human form of God, then we can look to Jesus' life over and over to see tangible examples of love in the world. He embodied love. He spoke about a reality that people often were not engaged in or aware of, the reality that love saw. That is why so many things He did actually confused others. They did not see through eyes of love. Everything Jesus said and did was laced in love that was being communicated to Him through His Spirit from the Father. We have the *same* relationship to the Father through the Holy Spirit!

Another passage that guides us is 1 Corinthians 13, which describes what love is and what it does. If we apply this to Jesus, we get a new revelation of who Jesus is to the world. Jesus is patient and kind, He does not dishonor others, He is not self-seeking, He is not easily angered, and He does not keep records of wrongs. Jesus always protects, trusts, hopes, and perseveres. Jesus never fails. This means that when we speak with love, genuine love, the love that God sees, we can never fail!

We see this played out over and over in the Scriptures. Peter denied Jesus in the most crucial moment, but Jesus did not keep records of wrongs, and He always hoped. This transformed Peter. After denying Christ, Peter went back to his old life as a fisherman. Jesus sought him out, helped him realign to God's love, and then Peter went on to be the rock on which the church was built. Think of that! One encounter with love is the reason we have churches today.

In Jesus' day people often assumed that those with physical ailments were living in sin or that God had cursed them. Jesus did not see that. Jesus approached them and, looking into His Father's intention and heart, saw them as healed, forgiven, and wholly loved.

When Jesus saw that the hungry crowds gathered around Him needed food, He was motivated by love to perform a miracle that caused more than enough food to appear.

We see the love of Jesus with the woman at the well. An

outcast in her society, she was restored to a place of dignity and honor, and then told her whole village about God's love.

We see the love of God intervene when a woman was going to be stoned for adultery. Jesus brought a new perspective that saved her life.

We see the love in Jesus when He told a story showing that an unsaved person, a Samaritan, could love and care for the needs of others and be more in tune with God's heart than people who believed in God and were preoccupied with self and religious acts. When you feel the genuine love of God, you no longer feel a false responsibility to religious acts, but you feel real responsibility to love. Even people with no formal relationship with God can feel Him and sense true aspects of Him, before they even know Him personally. He gives love freely to all.

PROCESS, PATIENCE, AND BUILDING INTIMACY WITH GOD

Sometimes the effects of love can take a lot of time, which means we must be patient and endure with hope. It can be hard, because if you're like me, you hate process. We want instant results and a formula that says, "If I do this one loving thing, I can control this person and make him or her become the person I think is best accepted by God." And yet God spent thousands of years pursuing the heart of the Israelites, and that pursuit is still not over. God is seen in the process as much as the instantaneous. He loves to condition us to His nature and help us know His heart more deeply, and that's why He doesn't always do things directly and instantaneously.

There have been times I've said to Him, "God, why do You talk to me in parables? I hate parables. They're the worst things in the world. Why are You doing this to me?" I'm not very patient (just ask my wife). God eventually showed me that He likes to speak in parables because He can reveal the nature of His heart through a story. If He speaks to us directly, we might take His message as a hard-and-fast principle and apply it without love. When He gave the children of Israel rules to follow and boundaries to respect, things didn't always go well. Even if people technically obeyed the law, they often did so with the wrong heart attitude. They did not do it with hearts aligned with God's, and so it became oppressive.

In Matthew 23:2–4 Jesus said (and remember it was Love Himself who was speaking), "The teachers of the law and the Pharisees sit in Moses' seat. So you must be careful to do everything they tell you. But do not do what they do, for they do not practice what they preach. They tie up heavy, cumbersome loads and put them on other people's shoulders, but they themselves are not willing to lift a finger to move them."

Jesus continued to warn about hypocrisy, saying in verse 15, "Woe to you, teachers of the law and Pharisees, you hypocrites! You travel over land and sea to win a single convert, and when you have succeeded, you make them twice as much a child of hell as you are."

We often think hypocrisy is saying one thing and doing another, and that is one accurate definition. We can also consider hypocrisy to be any act or word that violates love. This would be whenever we do not take the time to look at a situation with God, to see through His eyes of love, which He has given us. Honestly, I think that is the ultimate definition of hypocrisy. You can do something good for God, you can perform or preach or serve, but if it is not done with love, it is hypocritical.

Jesus taught that the Christian faith starts in the life of the heart, that it doesn't hinge on following specific detailed laws. He said we are actually free from the legalism of law without relationship. Through the price Jesus paid on the cross and the gift of the Holy Spirit, we can have everlasting connection to God.

When Jesus spoke in parables, He was revealing the Father's nature, inviting people to interpret them and figure out who He was through relationship. People who were used to the rules and regulations of the law were confused because He used parables more than direct discourse to communicate His principles. And they didn't understand why He spoke not only to believers and Hebrews but also to unbelieving crowds. He didn't lay it out simply by saying, "If you follow Me and My three steps to success, I will make you third in command." That would've been so much easier.

Most of us have had times when we wonder, *Why aren't You speaking to me in ways I understand, God?* The disciples did too. In John 16 Jesus spoke figuratively and then followed up with a little more explanation, and the disciples basically said, "Finally, You're speaking in ways that are clear, that we can understand." But who changed? Jesus never changed in the way He was talking to them. If you look at what He was saying, it was still parabolic and it was giving them the ability to know His deep thoughts. They now had become familiar with His nature and were beginning to understand what He was saying. They had spent time becoming familiar with His heart and, as a result, had been transformed through a relationship with love.

There's a powerful nature that God wants you to become familiar with as well. There's something He wants to impart deep inside you that's as real as any friendship you've ever had, and it's even deeper because it comes from within instead of outside you. One of the reasons His voice so often comes through impressions in your own thought life should actually encourage you: He truly lives within you. He speaks to your inner self even more than what we see in the Old Testament, when God's voice was audible or people had external visions. Those things might still happen today, but the majority of ways people who love God hear His voice is through impressions, intuition, coming from deep within. He is the voice of love within you.

Once you pursue this, everything will change for you.

Until you do, though, you'll probably pursue position, entitlement, resources, and the American dream in the Christianized form. It will feel as if you're using everything around you to teach an object lesson, including hearing God's voice for other people. With people who are not in the faith yet, your mission likely will be salvation alone—not to know them, care about them, see them the way God originally dreamed of them, or recognize that they are the joy that was set before Jesus, which created faith in Him to endure the cross (Hebrews 12:2). Instead, you'll look at evangelistic numbers to gain another notch in your belt or as a perceived success in your religious belief system. To the people you're trying to reach, it will feel like the bad kind of multilevel marketing to them (which you'd know well if you've ever been in a greed-based network marketing meeting). It won't feel like love or empowering people toward transformation.

OFFERING GOD'S LOVE TO OTHERS

People can sense an agenda with strings attached from a mile away. Loving as Jesus does will create an agenda, but its point is to create attachment and connection to God before anything else. Even when people don't accept it, it doesn't mean that they are unworthy of your time. This has been one of the most dysfunctional things that breaks the connection of true Christian love, because it creates an *us versus them* dynamic. But Jesus came to earth because God loves everyone on this planet. "God so loved the world that he gave his one and only Son, that whoever believes in him shall not perish but have eternal life" (John 3:16). We should treat everyone with honor, as though they are worthy of that price, even if they ultimately don't choose it.

Jesus said to many people, "Follow Me." Some of them replied, "I can't." One of the rich men said, "I can't do what You're asking me to do. I can't give everything I have to the poor." Jesus' response was basically, "Yeah, it's hard for someone like you to do that." After that man didn't accept Jesus' invitation to follow Him, Jesus didn't look at him and say, "I hate you. Depart from Me, you snob!" or, "To hell with you!" Instead, He reached out in love to understand, validate, and accept the man's response, saying, "It is easier for a camel to go through the eye of a needle" (Matthew 19:24). He meant, "This is a really hard thing, what I'm asking you to do."

I feel like we're afraid to love people because we're afraid that we'll be aligned with their bad choices. We refuse to accept people the way Jesus did. He never considered loving someone to be a blemish on His reputation, even if they had a bad one, because His love had no boundaries. Because we haven't seen this kind of love modeled more, there are parts of us that have detached from looking at what God's doing, which is a primary responsibility we have as Christians. We are to focus on what God's doing and then dwell in it. Worship Him. Praise Him for what He's doing. Be present with what He's doing. Connect to what He's doing.

Is there something else we need to do or get in order to connect with what God's doing and bring His love to the world? First Corinthians 4:8 reminds us, "You already have all you need. You already have more access to God than you can handle. . . . You're sitting on top of the world—at least God's world—and we're right there, sitting alongside you!" (THE MESSAGE).

God has provided access to Himself. If we feel we don't have power to fulfill our Christian calling, the only thing we're lacking is connection to what God is already doing, what He is already seeing, and what He is inviting us to move into and speak into so that He can transform it into what He intended it to be. The whole world is waiting for us to tell them what God is doing. Because God is good. And people want good in the world today.

NOT LETTING FEAR, JUDGMENT, OR RIGID EXPECTATIONS INTERFERE

Unfortunately, many Christians and public religious figures have been talking for a long time about what He's not doing. They've been sending messages of judgment, saying, "This is who God's not. This is what He's not doing. Your choices make you unfit for God, you're a liar, you're going to hell. That is bad, this is an idol. That is false religion, this is deception, that is evil. It's all going to hell and going to be destroyed!"

I do not believe that is what God is speaking. God is love. Yes, God judges rightly, but first, God wants to transform through love. I always think of Nineveh and Jonah when I think of this. God's plan is never destruction; it is redemption and love.

Hearing God's love for others is not just about them. It equips and helps you to be aligned with God and understand Him. You'll see more of what God sees every day as you learn to look with greater love. You will be able to see how He made things and people to be from the beginning.

I have changed so much since I've allowed God to bring love alive in me. It's almost unbelievable to me how, in the past, I didn't allow my heart to love people because of fear, and because the strength of my convictions and opinions was greater than the strength of my love. Some of my opinions didn't come out of the inspiration of love; they came out of what I thought was right and wrong.

Right and wrong will always war against love, because of the Tree of Life and the Tree of the Knowledge of Good and Evil. Life focuses on what God's doing and where He's loving. Knowledge of good and evil focuses on what's bad and what's good. It's knowledge that is outside the context of relationship.

Consider hearing a tabloid about your best friend's weaknesses that may have some truth in it. But when you have a relational connection to his or her whole story, you don't judge the person the same way you would otherwise, because love sees everything in the context of relationship. You see your friend's good and evil, and think, *Oh, that's evil. I still love him fully anyway. I just need to stay aware of that and will have to put up some new boundaries.* You know you're mature when evil doesn't keep you from loving. And if you start to mature in that, God will speak to you in such clear ways. His "Father's heart voice" will begin to transform people's lives through you.

Years ago, I had a spiritual encounter about the land I have felt called to live in, Los Angeles. God showed me what seemed like hundreds of thousands of faces of the diverse people there and filled my heart with love for them. I sensed that they were part of my mission. I could tell God's heart was wrapped around that city, and I felt like mine was too. The Lord said to me, "Thank you for loving who I love." As I was seeing those faces, He was expanding my heart to love.

I'm convinced that if you want to have a great impact on humanity—aka what the Bible calls "harvest"—you have to have a great love. You have to let God fill you with love for the people you are called to. You also have to grasp that they're His in the Spirit before you have authority with them, or else you will have only a limited authority.

I said earlier that in the past there were things holding me back from loving greatly. An obstacle for me was having particular expectations about what knowing and following Jesus should look like. Having rigid expectations is also what kept the Pharisees and Jewish leaders from experiencing Jesus as the Son of God when He came to earth. They had a specific expectation of who the Messiah would be, and as a result, they actually ended up missing Him! They did not realize Jesus was Love; they thought their savior would be a warrior king. They did not look through the eyes of love; they looked through the lens of their own understanding. And this is the same sickness we see in the Western church today: a greater dependency on man's wisdom than on God's love.

If we take an honest look at ourselves, however, we're often quick to do the same thing the Pharisees did. When have we crucified what Jesus wants to do? How often do we sacrifice the power He wants to bring to us and our world, simply because we're afraid to look through the eyes of love? We look through the eyes of our own minds and use Scripture to try to justify hate or uncomfortable feelings. Those who crucified Jesus also used Scripture to try to justify their actions, but they totally missed it! We do not have to keep missing it. Love is always there, ready to embrace us, teach us, and show us a more excellent way.

PROPHECY IS GOD'S LOVE RELEASED

I believe that hearing from God and using the gifts associated with that, those which the apostle Paul explained, is the fastest way to reveal the love nature of God to others. And He wants to give those tools to all of us. Those gifts are called the word of wisdom, the word of knowledge, and the word of prophecy, all of which fall in the category of prophetic ministry. A simpler way to say it is hearing God's voice for the world around us.

Revelation 19:10 says, "It is the Spirit of prophecy who bears testimony to Jesus." The testimony of what God's love does on the earth defines the spirit of prophecy. Prophecy is not separate from love. First Corinthians 14:4 tells us that prophecy is for edification, which means building up. In its truest, purest form, prophecy is God's love released in a way that edifies people, moving them into being who He wants them to be. It is seeing others with God's lens of truth and faith and hope, and giving them an invitation into that reality God already sees for them.

If you want to bring a prophetic encounter to the world around you, you'll need to have an encounter with the God of love first. You'll need to have deep, ongoing encounters of intimacy and connection with Him. It will have to be rooted in personally knowing God and His love, or, as 1 Corinthians tells us, it will come to nothing. God doesn't just give us information. He shares His heart and His nature with us.

For a season in my life, there were times the only prophetic word God would give me for people was that He loved them. But surprisingly, many people were deeply touched by this. They experienced the love in the word, and it went from a head knowledge to a heart knowledge, and it had power to transform them. "God loves you" is really what every single prophetic word is about, and it is powerful by itself.

But without love, even if the prophetic word is correct, even if you get words of knowledge about a person's name, place of birth, and everything about him or her, if you do not see love when you look at the person, you really do not see anything true at all. The word may feel exciting, but it will not bring transformation. Everything that has to do with the kingdom of heaven becomes available through a relationship with the God of love.

One of my favorite things about prophecy is that it connects you directly to the heart of God and the heart of people. When I experience it, I feel instantly connected to people, and it's so rewarding to feel their value. I feel as if I'm part of their journey, part of their story. Prophecy makes you feel as if you're in some of people's best moments, because these are the moments when God is revealing His loving nature in the most physical way. All of a sudden I will find myself standing in a monumental, defining moment, when a person grasps their true identity and God's love for them, and there's nothing like it. It's such a beautiful experience that you get addicted to the love of God in those moments.

Another wonderful thing about being around people who see you with love is that you forget who you were never meant to be. You forget your self-hatred, shame, and fear. You live in your true identity more easily. We will discuss this more in a later chapter.

I hope you've seen in this chapter that as people who love God, Christians need to be connected to our good Father. That's the heart of the prophetic. It's connecting others—through language, in imagery, in ideas, in words, in art, in music—to the heart of the good Father. God wants to reach people's hearts!

In the next couple of chapters I will establish a framework for how to speak God's words of love and the importance of having a relational context in prophecy. Then I will explore a variety of areas of life where God is bringing transformation and share many accounts of the amazing things I have seen God's love do in my life and in the lives of my friends.

2

SPEAKING GOD'S WORDS OF LOVE

For more than a decade, our church has reached out to the homeless in Los Angeles and, at times, street youth in Hollywood. One day I went to visit one of the outreach centers and was looking for a place to park. When I cut through an alley, I saw two teen boys—seeing them not only with my natural eyes but with my spiritual eyes. I drove closer to them and said from my car window, "Hey guys, can I talk to you for a second?"

They immediately thought I was going to proposition them as prostitutes and said that they were not into that. I explained that I was a pastor, that I saw one of them was crying, and that I wanted to talk to them about their lives and dreams. They came closer to my car, and I stepped out and asked what was happening. One of them had just received terrible news about a family member back home. He didn't have the money to go there, nor did he want to visit the family he had run away from. He had come to Hollywood to become an actor but ended up on the streets.

I could sense that God had these young men's hearts open and vulnerable. I asked the one who had been crying, "What do you want to do with your life?"

"I used to want to be an actor, but now I know that's not my path," he answered. "It's not because I didn't make it yet, but because it's just not me. I don't know what I want, and I have nowhere to go."

I could see this homeless runaway youth not only in his current condition but through the love of God. I could see his potential, his hard work ethic, his value and worth. "Let's ask God together to see if He will show you if He has any options for you," I suggested. "He is really good at giving purpose and meaning."

"I don't think God would want me. I haven't exactly been a good person to my family. Plus, I've been doing drugs." He patted his backpack.

"I don't think God cares about who you are not. I think He cares about who you are. He made you and loves you, even when you don't choose Him. Let's just ask." I smiled.

So we prayed together, all three of us. I said, "God, will You show my new friend here something that You have made him for that will bring his heart alive?"

After a few awkward minutes, I asked the young man, "Did anything come into your mind?"

"No," he said, disappointed. His friend was ready to move

on from the conversation, no doubt taking me as a quack since it didn't work. But then he said, "Well, I did think about how much I love coffee. I have since I was three. I'm really good at making it and started working as a barista in my hometown when I was thirteen. We even won a few awards. I would *love* to work as a barista again!"

It's crazy how often people discount what God is putting inside of them. I just asked a specific question, and God gave a specific answer, but because it came from within, this young man had discounted it.

"Don't you think it would be worth pursuing again?" I asked. "God gave you a love for creativity, for making things, and coffee was an outlet He used to bring you alive. Why don't we ask Him how you can pursue it now, so you can find a place of passion again?"

He was so excited. We prayed again, and he clearly received direction about a coffee shop that he visited regularly down the street from the youth shelter he was staying in. He had built a great rapport with the manager there, and he couldn't wait to talk to him.

At this point he was no longer a homeless youth with bad news from home. He was a young man filled with hope, potential, and a recreated sense of purpose, all because he felt seen. When I found a runaway in an alley, I could have seen him with my natural eyes, and maybe had compassion and given him some money or a meal. But what he really needed was connection to the love of the One who gives love.

God has a different way of looking at things than we do, and one of the greatest things that Jesus did was give this perspective away to humanity. He showed us how God sees things.

A PERSPECTIVE SHIFT TURNS
SORROW TO JOY

One day I was having lunch with some of my good friends, and several of their staff members had joined us. A man sitting across from me kept my mind occupied.

At the same time, and I didn't know why, I also kept thinking about how my mom and dad had lost my brother late in the month of October, and for a long time afterward that was a dark time of year for my mom specifically. Then one year God poured healing and love into her, and October was never a time of grieving and mourning again. For me, October had become a time when I could feel the presence of God's love and recognize special moments. It was almost like God was bringing blessings to redeem the time of year when my brother had passed, so that I could focus on His goodness.

For some reason, looking at the man across from me brought all of this to mind.

I asked him, "Can I share something of a spiritual story with you?" He was curious and open. I told him the story of my family's loss, but I added something that I felt I heard from God: "God wants you to know that you and your family are going to have redemption for whatever bad things have happened in October. Every year from now on, you are going to see His goodness."

He was shocked. "I had an affair twelve years ago, and my wife found out on October 22," he said. "We walked through a long healing journey, and she forgave me, but that date in October has always been one we want to get past. I have never thought of it as a date to look forward to." He paused and considered.

"But I really should, because our story has changed so much in twelve years. God has given us a victorious marriage. And by sharing our experience with other couples, we've helped many other marriages heal too."

I love how God used one simple word to change this man's perspective on something significant in his life. This mental shift introduced the potential for October to be a reminder of the victory of living in restoration instead of the pain of a past trial.

BEGINNING IN THE PROPHETIC MINISTRY

These types of stories may sound amazing, powerful, and supernatural. But God designed us all to hear His voice. I find it almost funny that people are always asking me how to move in the prophetic gifts, or what I call prophetic ministry, because I often still feel unqualified and as if I don't know what I'm getting myself into. We should all feel that way, because technically, we are not qualified.

The good news is that love needs no qualifications or degrees to empower it to be effective. God loves to use us in places where we don't expect it, when we're just available and saying yes to God's heart. God crosses any barrier to say, "I am Love, and here is something I have in My heart for you." And it changes people from the inside out.

So, when people ask me, "How did you get here? How did God raise you up?" I laugh. I never wanted to be a poster boy for the Hearing God Ministry. I've never felt "more special" than anyone else. There were no angels announcing my birth or words from God about who I would be before I was born. I am just a normal guy, and thankfully, God wants to use normal people like you and me.

Also, this has not been a miracle gift for me. I have gotten prophetic words wrong—not just a few times, but many times. And I have had to put my pride aside when I've gotten it wrong. I've had to learn how to do this ministry, just like anyone else, and I've had to be willing to invest time in practicing.

In the beginning what really helped me was just focusing on what a person loved most, what he or she was most passionate about, and what God had put in his or her heart. I would try to hear God on these things, and if I got them wrong, no harm done. To others it would just sound like a random question, not a missed prophetic word. For example, I might ask, "Do you like football?" instead of saying, "The Lord says you like football." Then if he or she answered no, I wouldn't have created an awkward situation for that person.

Even if I did get it wrong, if I was coming from love, it opened the door for conversation and the beginning of a connection point to talk or to build a conversation that can lead to a friendship relational process, or the way you build relationships, which can be just as meaningful. It's not about me being right or wrong. It is all about relationship.

So what do I do to nurture relationship? Let's say the person says no to liking football. Well, then I can simply follow up with, "What do you enjoy doing?" And I listen to and appreciate the things God gave him or her to enjoy. Sometimes the interest and excitement I show about the things a person loves mean just as much as a prophetic word. This is why I have come to realize that social skills are very important to God, and that learning how to interact with others respectfully is important if you want to grow in the prophetic. We will discuss this in depth in the next chapter, "Revelation Is About Relationship."

PERSISTENCE, NOT PERFECTION

When people ask me how I got to where I am, I say it was by being willing to say yes over and over and over, and not letting my heart get weary. I have friends who spent more time in ministry than I have, and they're not even Christians today. They're not even walking with God anymore because they lost focus on love and the excitement of their relational connection to God and others. Instead they got stuck in the performance of religion and sometimes got hurt by serving a structure of ministry or church instead of the relational heart of God and people.

Now I didn't do anything special; I just practiced and stayed the course, saying to God, "I'm going to be faithful. If You tell me to do it, I'm going to obey You, no matter what. It may not be pretty or awesome, but I'm going to keep going forward. I'm in this for the long haul. I am going to keep my love in focus as my primary goal."

For me, and I think this would be true for 99.9 percent of us, before it was really awesome, it was *not* really awesome. For a while. And then all of a sudden, God popped in, and then it started to get better and better. To walk in the prophetic love of God, we have to have faith, and *obedience* is another word for faith.

And, again, love is not about being right. So if you're going into the prophetic with an Old Testament mentality that says, "You have to be right, or else you're not from God!" you have it all wrong. We are under a new covenant that is greater than right or wrong, and the new covenant is love. We are now judged by love, not performance.

So, sometimes God takes us on a relational journey where we think we've missed it, but actually, His main goal is simply for us to go to Him. He wants us to see ourselves not as performers but as His friends and children, who are allowed to get it wrong and accept grace. This experience does so much for our relationship with God—more than if we always get it right.

It is the same in human relationships. When things are going well, people may get along, but it is in the hard times, in trials and frustrations and insecurity, when we have the chance to be vulnerable with each other. Then together we can trust God and know that, no matter what happens, we can depend on Him.

Also, I am convinced that some people prematurely give up on hearing God for others because they have never accepted God's grace and unconditional love for themselves. This will stunt anyone's progress, because we cannot give to others what we do not have.

LOVING FOR THE SAKE OF LOVING

Once you have received God's love yourself and your heart is committed to persistence, you need to check your motivation and to clarify your focus and role.

There are many people who love but have separated

themselves from everything unlovely. They live in a Christian bubble and think that's what God has designed them to do. And so they're afraid of people who are not already experiencing God's love. They know perfect love casts out fear, but their fear of man is still greater than their faith in God's love.

The entertainment industry has been my training ground for this. I meet many people of radical faith—not faith in God, but faith in what they're going to accomplish in their lives. If some Christians spent time around them, they'd think the first thing they need to do is convert them. If the non-Christians wouldn't convert, then the Christians would abandon them. I see that as acting out of fear.

I've had to separate myself from having to be on a missional journey to make all the people I minister to believe what I believe. I've had to separate myself from the agenda to save them, because that agenda actually violates love. Love is its own agenda, and the moment you put an agenda on top of that, you're violating that love agenda. Of course I want everyone to get saved; I've led hundreds of people to Jesus, and I'll continue to do that. But my interaction with people is not hinged on the issue of their salvation.

We all have to learn this principle in order to move into hearing God: His agenda is love, and salvation is the fruit of love. I've had to force myself not to put my goal of converting people first. I've had to learn not to try to change people artificially.

Back in 2006 a bunch of young guys lived with me. I thought my role was to be their mentor, father figure, and discipler, but they didn't really want any of that. They wanted a friend they could process their lives with. They wanted to be empowered to make their own decisions, even if they were stupid decisions.

They didn't want me managing them, but they still wanted relationship. It's similar to the process of an adult helping a teenager try to figure out his or her identity by supporting his or her choices instead of trying to control every behavior.

For a while I felt like a failure when one of these young men made a bad decision that I could have helped him avoid, had he only listened. They were trying to figure out their own theology, identities, and lives, and whenever I tried to help in an unwanted way, they felt my agenda more than my love and would back away.

At one point during this time, God said to me, "I'm putting you around these people who I love so much because I want to teach you that love doesn't control."

If love is offered, it will blossom, no matter how many bad decisions might be involved in a situation. Love itself is strong enough to cause a change to happen from inside a person, which then can change behavior. After all, during Jesus' time on earth, He went after the heart first, and behavior was a result of heart change. He had such grace for people's processes that we don't have. We want a principle to be followed and the proof of action to back it up, whether or not a person's heart has changed.

Many people throughout history hated the kings and queens they served but continued pleasing those leaders because they feared for their lives. Jesus didn't want fear-based loyalty. He came to restore us to God's relational plan. Our perspectives can be so black-and-white that we don't realize love with good boundaries can have a lot of gray areas, because love accepts all things. If my job isn't to manage you but instead is to bring accountability through relationship, then my whole agenda changes.

FIVE ROADBLOCKS TO HEARING GOD FOR OTHERS

God is always speaking, and we often do not even know He is speaking. It's like we're in a world with free Internet access but don't have our devices turned on to connect. That does not mean the connection is not available, all around us, at all times. God makes it possible for us to reach out and receive all the information we need to bring love to the world.

The lack of a healthy relational process can get in the way of walking in the fullness of love's power and receiving what God has for us. This is the first of five roadblocks I see keeping people from hearing the love God is speaking for others.

There are a million things you can say and do to stimulate a conversation with someone and invite him or her to view you as a safe place. A lot of times a person will even bring up an issue God has been preparing you to address with him or her, but still you can't sidestep the relational process. Each situation is different, so it won't play out the same way each time. You may carry prayer for someone for a long season, or you may talk to a person right away, but the guiding principle is the same: it's about love.

This will affect how you approach every interaction. I used to be more direct with people when I felt that God was speaking to me about something important in their lives. I was quick to confront and say things in a way that were relationally violating.

"How's the divorce going?"

"Do you need help with this specific sin God showed me that you've been involved in?"

I would confront people on life issues they weren't even asking me to be a part of. I had to learn that, even though God might show me something, I should only do and say what I see Him doing and saying.

At one point God said to me, "I'm showing you some things to invite you into the conversation I'm having, but you need to pray. Sometimes as you wait, a person may invite you into My process with them."

For example, one day I discovered that an acquaintance was dealing with some hard-core pornography issues. I had no leadership or management in his life, and I hadn't had enough face time with him to talk to him about something so personal. I knew it wasn't my job to do anything about it except pray for him.

Even Jesus waits to be invited into our hearts and our lives. He does not bulldoze His way in. But He is ready and willing to step in with His love at any point, just as He said in Matthew 11:28–30: "Come to me, all you who are weary and burdened, and I will give you rest. Take my yoke upon you and learn from me, for I am gentle and humble in heart, and you will find rest for your souls. For my yoke is easy and my burden is light."

At a later time I saw this acquaintance again, and we had the chance to have a private conversation. He began to share how his marriage was almost wrecked by disconnection and that, in his pain, he could not turn off his long-term pornography addiction. He said, "I never have shared this with anyone. Maybe it's because I was never ready to deal with it, but it's costing too much."

I shared that God had showed me this issue in his life, and that, because of God's love, I had been praying for him for months.

He was so amazed, and tears came to his eyes. The fact that someone had been praying for him when he was too ashamed and afraid to open up to anyone, and the fact that he wasn't alone, was too much for his heart. It broke open under the weight of God's love.

He now knew God wanted to help him. He realized this wasn't only a natural issue but a spiritually rooted issue, one that God's love wanted to uproot. God wanted to give him the connection he needed with his wife, which this addiction was a substitution for (and a bad one).

I prayed with him and gave him the number of a therapist he could call. He felt true hope about conquering an issue that had been a lifelong battle.

Shame will never transform us to be more like God. But love can. Imagine if I had simply blurted out, "Why are you using so much pornography? Don't you know that's bad for you?" It would have been shaming and prevented me from being able to support him. It would have violated love. But because I led with love, it made a way for transformation instead of provoking defensiveness or shame.

The second roadblock to hearing God's love for others is the assumption that hearing specific things from God is somehow attached to the New Age or psychic community. It's scary when that is our only context for understanding how someone would be able to hear or predict something about a person. But one important thing to remember is that the Devil cannot create; only God can create. The Enemy has all of history, which is imprinted spiritually in a realm that sits just beside ours. Everything we do is visible, everything that happens is visible, everyone who dies and lives is visible. Angels know it, God knows it, and the Enemy knows it, because those kinds of truths don't diminish.

Psychics, or any other spiritual expressions not connected to

Jesus, are just coming across those truths available in the spiritual realm. Maybe they're interacting with demonic beings, but they don't have a relationship with God, so they can't see what's in His heart. Again, the Devil did not create the spiritual realm; God did.

And God created us to be able to hear details about people's lives and futures through the construct of relationship with Him through His Spirit, whom Jesus sent us at the resurrection. People apart from Jesus can predict things and even possibly be right, but if it is not done with love, the Bible says it profits nothing.

To Christians, prophecy is transformational love that is shared through specific details about the future, or words of knowledge about who people are. It moves people forward into their spiritual destinies, resolves spiritual issues, transforms possibilities, and aligns us with God's will.

To other spiritual communities, prophecy is simply prediction for the sake of encouragement. It isn't transformational in focus and has no power to bring true spiritual resolution, because that only happens through God. They are bringing about spiritual words without spiritual power, spiritual insight without God's relational heart framing it. Even if a psychic gets everything right for someone, hearing facts about that person and details about his or her future, that information will not last.

God, however, is the origin of the things that will last: faith, hope, and love (1 Corinthians 13:13). Even if a psychic's word has the appearance of love, it is not coming from the source of love, so it is not actually helpful or empowering to a person. If it does not come from love, it can create bondage.

People who are the most destructive to prophetic ministry are those who don't go beyond discerning a word, or basically, gathering facts. They won't go to the next step, which is saying, *God, I do not just want to know facts. I want to know what You see when You look at this fact and how I can love this person as You do.*

On the other hand, even a wrong word with love still can have a good result, because love never fails.

The third roadblock I want to discuss is focusing on our performance and perfection instead of on love. While we are trying to hear the voice of God, we interpret a message that is wrong, or we are given a spiritual message from another believer that is wrong, and then it takes root in our hearts as disappointment or frustration at others or God. To really hear God, we have to be willing to hear what love is saying, even messages that feel disappointing. The Bible reminds us that we may be able to hear God yet not actually understand or apply it to our lives.

Jesus said to people who were open spiritually but not rooted and grounded in mature love, "You will be ever hearing but never understanding; you will be ever seeing but never perceiving. For this people's heart has become calloused; they hardly hear with their ears, and they have closed their eyes. Otherwise they might see with their eyes, hear with their ears, understand with their hearts and turn, and I would heal them" (Matthew 13:14–15).

God does not see the way we see, even when we look at the exact same situation. During Jesus' time on earth, most people did not see Him through the eyes of love. They rejected Him, who was love in the flesh, because they did not have love in them to help them see. In Matthew 11:19 Jesus said people thought He was "a glutton and a drunkard, a friend of tax collectors and sinners." They assumed His willingness to eat and drink with the lost was about gluttony, when it really was about love. Right fact, wrong understanding.

We've all had similar experiences in our own lives. Maybe there was a time you talked with someone you trusted about a hard situation, and they saw the situation differently than you did. As you listened to that person, you could change your perspective and align it with a higher truth that benefitted you. For example, maybe you saw someone trying to hurt you by ignoring you, and you were offended. But then you talked with a mentor, and he or she explained how that person was busy and running late to a meeting at the time. When you realized you had not been ignored, you became open to restoring the false image you had about that person. Maybe there was a time you felt stuck in a situation and didn't think of a solution until a friend pointed out something to you. This is what God can and will do for us!

One of the names Jesus used for the Holy Spirit was Counselor (John 14:26 HCSB). He is the best life and relationship coach in the world, and the Bible is full of relational truth that can help you immensely.

If disappointment and frustration have been holding you back from hearing God, I want to challenge you to invite Him into that, so you can look at your situation with His eyes. When God looks at a situation, He sees redemption. He sees opportunities for you to grow so you can flourish. He sees how you can have hope and faith and how your relationship with Him can become stronger than your perspective of the hurtful or confusing situation. If someone gave you a word and got it wrong, seek God about it. Ask Him to speak to your heart about it so you can see how He wants to love you and redeem the situation.

The fourth roadblock to hearing God is the fear of mistakes. It's a toxic fear in our lives because it doesn't line up with what God sees. Love covers not only a multitude of sins but also a multitude of mistakes. You can still hear God in helpful ways and impact people for good by what you say and do, even if you get some things wrong! People want to be loved by you more than they want you to be right about everything. That love ultimately has the bigger impact in their lives.

If you reflect on your own life, you will probably see that has been true for you. You would rather have a friend who loves you and expresses that love than a friend who is always right. (In fact, a friend who cares more about being right than loving you does not sound like a good friend at all!) As I've said before, we have to shift our focus from trying to perform in the prophetic to trying to love through the prophetic.

I'd say trying is one of God's favorite things. If you have a son or daughter, think of him or her trying something new. How wonderful is that? When my daughter is trying to cook in her toy kitchen, I think it's the most fantastic thing I've ever watched. She doesn't have to be perfect for me to enjoy watching her play. God's like that with us; He enjoys our processes. When you're trying to please Him, you can never fail. God looks at you and says, "Wow, I'm so proud of you. I see your heart. What you're doing is so beautiful." And He works all things for the good of those who love Him. You don't have to be right. He'll still work it out for your good if you keep your heart open.

Not long ago I was at an airport, and after I got my ticket, I walked up to a guy and said, "Are you working on a business deal in the tech world?"

He answered no.

"Okay, thanks," I said, feeling super insecure, which was stupid because God loves that I even tried.

"Why'd you ask?" the man asked me.

"I am a Christian and just felt in my heart that God has made you for some great opportunities, and one might be in the tech world."

"Wow, I'm impressed that you would try and talk to me about something you felt God was showing you," he replied. "Do you believe God can talk?"

What a great question, and one that never would have come up if I hadn't tried to engage him in conversation. We spent a while talking about his faith, his heart, and my life. It felt as if we were two old friends talking about something important. Since that conversation he has become open to Christianity and has even started attending a church. God used my willingness to take the time to show him care and to model relationship—something I am still growing in.

Sometimes there will not be a visible happy ending. Sometimes people will be mean to you and you will be persecuted. But keep in mind that God doesn't mind others getting offended. He may want to use you to deal with the offense in them so He can actually reach them, and it has nothing to do with you.

Other times you will get it wrong, and He may give you the opportunity to continue to love in a way that redeems it. Through that He may bring people closer to Him, bring them closer to trusting you, and restore hope.

For example, I once was having dinner with a group that included some long-term acquaintances. They told the group, "We need prayer and we need direction, but there isn't anyone in our sphere of life we trust right now."

Later I pulled them aside and said, "I would be glad to pray for you."

They seemed a little leery.

The next moment I remembered that I had prayed for them years before and had shared some words of prophecy with them. One was about a financial breakthrough that was going to come by a certain date.

I asked them, "Years ago when I prayed for you, did what I prophesied come true for you?"

They both looked at each other. Then the floodgates opened. Nothing anyone ever said to them had come true, and that word had been the most disappointing of all because they had really believed in me. They had been so sad about me and hearing God ever since.

I took responsibility and apologized. I told them how sorry I was that the word hadn't happened and that others hadn't either. I felt bad that they had walked through such a rocky road with hearing God's voice, but when we talked, a weight came off their shoulders.

I got the group of friends to pray for them, and people even prophesied some things, and they listened. You know what? The fact that I apologized and everyone shared messages of love with them broke a vicious cycle in their lives, and they had their first really good experience with God's voice. Taking responsibility in relationships is a huge key to growing in hearing God's voice, because love is accountable.

Finally, the fifth and biggest roadblock to listening to God and sensing His love for others is simply not being sure how to hear God and what God sounds like. As Christians, we know we get to hear from God, because that's how we got saved: He revealed Himself to us. We take our first major step in communicating with Him by giving Him our lives as we receive His. This divine exchange is communication, so it shouldn't be a far step to believe that the communication continues from there.

Once we are saved we are connected to God's heart through the Bible and through the Holy Spirit, who lives in us. First Corinthians 2:10–11 says the Holy Spirit connects the deepest, innermost thoughts of God's Spirit to ours, and that we have the perceptions, or mind, of Christ. This means that the way most people often hear God is through their inner thought processes.

But how do we know what is from God and what is from us? The answer comes by listening, practicing, and applying what you hear to real life. It isn't the most exciting or spiritual solution, but it's the truth.

You know what feels spiritual sometimes? Emotions. You know what feels spiritual other times? Hormones. You know what feels spiritual a lot of times? Opinions. Or knowledge. But there's something higher than all those things, and it's called revelation, or spiritual connection. We have to practice being aware of when it is God speaking and when it is one of the other common human processes happening within us.

Sometimes when we're trying to listen to God, we are really hearing our emotions. It feels almost the same. It's like a young man in church asking, *God, who am I going to marry?* He sees the prettiest girl, and to him, his hormones sound like Jesus saying, "That is her." No, friend, those are your hormones saying, *Please God, please God, please God, let her be the one.* That's totally different. But it can sound the same. Another example is when you're physically hungry for food, and you might feel as if the Lord wants you to eat, when it is just a normal appetite.

You can superspiritualize any of the voices of your inner processes. If you're hungry for something, you're going to create an answer out of that hunger. You have to be careful to identify whether you're doing that, and then discern and listen to what's in God's heart.

THREE REVELATORY GIFTS OF THE PROPHETIC MINISTRY

When people use the term *prophetic ministry*, they're referring to the revelatory gifts. As I mentioned in the last chapter, the three primary revelatory gifts are the word of wisdom, the word of knowledge, and the word of prophecy. Let's discuss each one.

First, a word of wisdom is basically revelation about what to do with other revelation, life mission, calling, purpose, and destiny. Have you ever noticed that when you get a revelation, it's not always a complete picture? Sometimes it sets your hope onto something. Maybe it's a revelation about what you're going to do in the future. Maybe it's about a business, your family, or something else, but you don't know what to do with it yet. A word of wisdom reveals how to position your current information, what perspective you should have.

It's what business leaders need when they have a vision or goal, but they need revelation on how they can actually implement it. I think words of wisdom are a type of revelation the world needs most right now because they make the most complicated things simple. They activate what's already inside of people. Even unsaved people have a sense of destiny and feeling, but they need a word of wisdom about what to do with what they're feeling inside.

Second, a word of knowledge is God's perspective about something that is current or past, something that is happening or has happened. It's information that makes people feel connected to the fact that God knows them, that they're known by heaven, that they're important. The word of knowledge isn't just information; it's knowledge that connects us to God's perceptions and inner thoughts.

You can have intuition or even spiritually discerned information, but that's not a word of knowledge. I can discern or even just psychologically read some things about you, such as, "You're artistic and creative." That just helps me to ask God about your life. But that's not necessarily a word of knowledge.

A word of knowledge is when it's God speaking, and He's helping a person understand that he or she was intimately thought of for millions of years before the present moment. It's God communicating to that person, "I know your name. I know where you live. I know the season you've been in, and I've been there every step of the way. I love you."

One time a prophet who didn't know my family said my family's names as part of a prophecy in front of thousands of people: "Larry and Staciae," he said, "you have a prophetic family. You have Shawn and Jen Sendifer." He was saying Cindy and Jennifer at the same time, who are my two sisters, but he couldn't figure it out. Then he said, "I don't know. Cindy or Jenny or something," which was both of them. It was perfect.

Then he continued, "And God's going to use your household to bring salvation to whole households." It was so beautiful and such a simple word as he called out all my family by name. I knew that God knew us. We were important to heaven. That was amazing. Of course, I already knew that because I was a

Christian, but it was powerful for somebody to call me out and define God's love for me in a moment like that.

Words of knowledge can be so important because they can help strengthen people's faith that they are known by God. Ultimately, what people want to know is that they are known. We want to understand others and for them to understand us, and when that happens it creates connection. So when God does that for somebody through words of knowledge, it helps them set their faith on the truth that God is good. Then when you prophesy or give more revelation to that person, his or her heart is already completely open and able to receive it. I love that.

The same thing happens with words of knowledge in healing. If you say something like, "Somebody here has a left knee injury from a car accident" (and it's a word of knowledge that's accurate for somebody), then that person who has that injury will have full faith that he or she will be healed, even if that person didn't believe it when he or she walked into the room. All of a sudden that person thinks, *Oh my gosh, God knows my injury. He saw it happen, and He loves me enough to heal me.* It helps prepare someone to believe that God can heal his or her heart or other parts of his or her life. And this shows us the purpose of words of knowledge.

Words of knowledge require practice and can feel like a guessing game until you get them right. But when you do get them right, it is beautiful. They help people know that God knows who they are and what they need. When people see God communicate about them to someone else in an accurate and personal way, they are healed from loneliness and from the belief that God doesn't care. Their faith increases when they see God as a personal God, not a God somewhere far away. But the only way to grow as one who gives words of knowledge is literally to take a risk a thousand times. Over the course of a thousand times, you'll figure out what's real, and you'll figure out how to reproduce that fruit over and over and over.

You're going to make lots of mistakes along the way. I've made lots and lots of mistakes! Nothing that can put me in prison (praise Jesus!), but still things that made me feel like an odd-ball. And that's hard. Sometimes we do not want to take a risk unless we know the reward. When Jesus is your reward, however, love will cover every risk you take. And if you get to know Him through your practice, you'll be rewarded really well.

Finally, the third primary revelatory gift, a word of prophecy, is a foretelling of what God wants to do. It's God's showing us His divine will. It creates a container of faith for God to do something significant in our lives in the future. It helps people feel connected to God in the now. When the Bible says that prophecy edifies, that means it helps someone feel the meaningfulness of his or her life. When the Bible says prophecy encourages, it creates encouragement for relationships, purpose, direction, and hardship in someone's journey. We see that hearing from God for others and sharing it becomes a huge source of nurturing to someone's connection with God. It grounds that person in spiritual truth that usually results in even more hunger for the Bible and time with God.

People often call all three of these types of revelatory gifts *a prophetic word* and don't actually know the skill set they're operating out of. But knowing the distinctions between them can help us practice each individual gift and expand its usefulness in our lives. We also might find that we have a particular strength in one.

PROPHECY SHOULD FEEL LIKE LOVE

Whatever revelatory gift is involved, remember this: The voice of God sounds like a friend. The voice of God sounds like a wise counselor. The voice of God sounds like someone who others, especially strangers, would want to hear from. A message from God sounds like something so good or so important that you can't help but give it away to a stranger.

Every time we engage in the prophetic, it is a direct communication from God's heart, which can transform and reset a person's entire foundation. That's such a huge responsibility, but it is also so profound. The Holy Spirit goes in the deepest parts of God's heart, and then He relates those thoughts to our hearts and minds. God says, "I don't see as you do. You need to learn to see as I see. I look at people and I'm happy to be with them." (Consider the prodigal son.)

John 3:17 says, "God did not send his Son into the world to condemn the world, but to save the world through him." Jesus came to put the world right again. That is what He did with His life, and that is what the prophetic ministry does. It's not here to convict the world of sin or tell people what they've done wrong; the Holy Spirit does that individually for us. People don't need two Holy Spirits or for someone to try to be the Holy Spirit to them. They need someone to be Jesus to them.

Jesus came for everyone in the world, including those who have sinned "the worst." There's incredibly good news for them: Jesus loves them! God wants to use us to help them understand that love, and being close to His heart will drive us to do that.

Being close to Jesus also involves sharing in His sufferings, and His heart suffers for injustice on the earth. He never looks away from injustice, and He intercedes before the throne for those who suffer. There will be times when He will share His deep heart of justice with you.

Whether you're sharing exciting news with the lost or you're carrying the burdens of the broken, your life will be full of meaning and purpose when you are focused on the heart of God.

I pray that as you read the following chapters that you would allow your heart to be challenged and that you would fight against anything that gets in the way of love. That you would be someone who tells the world who they are, not who they aren't. That you'd be able to focus on what God is doing, not on what He is not doing. That you would dwell on God's goodness and glory that has filled the earth.

3

REVELATION IS ABOUT RELATIONSHIP

It is in the context of our relationship with God and others that we experience love. Not only that, but love gains its power when it is shared.

Out of love God created man and woman for each other. He proclaimed, "It is not good for the man to be alone" (Genesis 2:18). In 1 John 4:19 we come to understand that "we love because he first loved us." God initiated a loving relationship with us and models for us what love does, how it looks, how it feels.

Seeing through God's eyes of love will help us have healthy relationships, both naturally and supernaturally. The eyes of love always look for relationship before agenda.

One way we can build a loving relationship with others is by valuing what they value. When we love God, we value what He values. To show God's love to others through the prophetic, we value what they value. When people feel like Christians treasure what they treasure, and that God treasures what they treasure, they'll come en masse to hear more about God.

God helped this concept hit home for me when I was at a big conference and I felt Him highlight a family to me. It was a mom, dad, son, and daughter. The daughter was about seven, and the son was about fourteen. They were sitting in the second row, reserved for the staff of the church, so I assumed they were somehow associated with the leadership. I couldn't have been more wrong.

I stopped my message and said to them, "I am having a spiritual picture for you, and I want to share it now for everyone here to hear."

What I didn't know was that ushers had brought them to that row because the church was so full. They weren't Christians and didn't know what a vision or spiritual picture was. The couple was also on the verge of divorce.

So the joke was on me. I expected them to be open to hear from God because of where they were sitting. Normally people are happy when I say I have a word for them from God, but when I looked at their faces, I was confused. *Wow, they don't look super happy right now. This is weird.* But I did feel God had spoken to me, so I said again, "I have a word for your family."

I can't even remember what the word was, but they did not seem impressed or receptive. In fact, the dad was giving me a look that said I should have a psychiatric evaluation. But this word was for them; it was not about me. So I was willing to adjust how I spoke or to do whatever I could to help them receive it.

Then I saw one more picture. It was even more absurd, but it felt like Jesus. He was totally aware of where their hearts were, and He was revealing to me something they valued.

I turned to the little girl and said, "I can see a picture of you holding something—your little pet, named Fluff-fluff. I'm sorry he died. But guess what? I see Jesus holding Fluff-fluff in His hands, like this," and I held my hands close to my heart. "He's holding Fluff-fluff and taking care of him. Fluff-fluff is in heaven with Jesus."

I looked back to the family, trying to read their nonverbal communication. I'd just given a risky, very specific word! Would they be angry that I was talking to her daughter about a pet? What if she didn't have a pet? What if their pet had not died yet? Who knows?

To my surprise the whole family began to cry—including the dad. I moved back into speaking my message, but afterward they came up to me. They told me the daughter's pet Fluff-fluff had just died. When he had died, the girl had asked her dad, "Did he go to heaven?"

The dad had answered, "No, honey, there is no heaven, and your pet didn't go there. There's no place for your pet to go. Animals just die, and that is it."

This had really wounded her heart. Kids are created to know and understand God, and there is a reason kids want to believe in heaven: it is true. To them, believing in heaven seems more right and natural than not believing in heaven.

If I'd been only looking at whether the dad had been right or wrong, I would have told the dad he was wrong. But when I looked at him through the eyes of love, I realized he wanted to offer his daughter what he considered to be valuable truth, which included his belief that God and heaven did not exist. His beliefs were broken, but even in that brokenness, his heart desired to do the best thing for his daughter and to be honest with her.

After I shared the word about Fluff-fluff, the dad started to feel convicted—and I hadn't said anything convicting. He knew there was no way for me to know about Fluff-fluff apart from God. I knew nothing about this family. They hadn't even planned on coming to this event where I was speaking, so I couldn't have talked to anyone to get information about them. No one could have told me about Fluff-fluff, how much the daughter valued her pet, or the impact that Fluff-fluff's death had on her heart—no one except God.

This young girl was hearing for the first time how much God loved what she loved, even more than she loved it, and how God had prepared a place for her with the things she loved. And of course, her parents loved and valued her, so they were deeply touched by God's love for her as well.

The dad realized that it had been his own disappointment in life that had caused him to become an atheist. This word helped to heal his own hurts as well.

Remember, things in this family were not going well. The couple was headed toward divorce, and this word brought hope and healing for other disappointments and areas of brokenness. The whole family became Christians that day, all because of a dead pet named Fluff-fluff. Not only that, the relationships between the family members were strengthened and could be restored to what God saw through His eyes of love when He looked at them. This experience opened their minds and hearts to a God who loves to bring restoration and hope.

This is why I just love the prophetic. It opens up our hearts and moves us past what we're able to think about on our own. We can begin with a mind-set that is not ready to change, or not even considering it, and suddenly, we can see an option for the future that we couldn't before.

HEARING ABOUT MARRIAGE AS A SINGLE PERSON

God does not, however, always give us the option we want. People often ask me to prophesy over relationships, especially about who someone should marry or when someone will meet his or her future spouse. Sometimes God does give those words, but it is rarely when people come with an agenda, asking for a word. God has His own agenda that He wants to talk about and bring us into. That doesn't mean our agenda isn't pertinent to Him, but when He is leading us or speaking to us, it is for our ultimate good. He will often not answer one of our questions because it's not as important as what He is curating in our lives at that time.

The riskiest things we can give words about are spouses, deaths, or babies. Relationships are the most important thing in life, so they also can create the biggest disappointments. If a prophetic word doesn't happen, then it can create a severe disconnect between people and God. It can also cause a person to miss the greatest blessing in his or her life. If someone chooses not to pursue the right person because he or she doesn't match up with a prophetic word, it can cause a lot of damage.

When I was in my teens and I wasn't secure in my true identity, I was like many young people in the church looking for God to tell me who I was supposed to marry. I was not asking for this out of fullness of my relationship with Him. I was asking out of curiosity and wanting this very defining relationship to develop, not knowing that God wanted to do so much more in my life before my marriage. I didn't know myself well or feel firm in who I was. I wasn't practiced in getting to know girls and figuring out what I liked and wanted. I didn't think I was strong or wise enough to make the right choice.

I think we want these types of words because they could let us skip building a healthy self-reliance and self-responsibility. We also could get out of the awkward relational pursuit process! Human relationships and self-connection is ultimately what our lives are all about, and God wants to nudge us in the right direction but also empower us to make great choices, including picking a spouse.

I tried to get God to tell me about my future spouse because I didn't know that I could be (or perhaps didn't want to be) empowered in my identity, my own development process, and my relational skills. I did not want to have to invest in understanding myself and understanding relationships. That was too hard! If I picked the wrong person, I felt I would've had to blame myself for not knowing it was the wrong person. But if God chose for me and it was a mess, then it would be His mess and I could just have faith in Him. My ego would not be bruised because I had done it for God, not myself.

But God told me, "Do not abdicate the responsibility I've given you. You have the right to choose your spouse, and I enjoy you when you make powerful choices. I made you to be an empowered individual. You're going to be ruling over the heavens with Me—not as My servant, but as My son and friend."

My wife, on the other hand, heard from God about me, but that is a whole other story she can tell.

It is the same with every single decision or relationship or purpose that we pursue in any context. When you understand that, it changes how you prophesy. You don't give words that are dangling carrots in front of people. Prophetic words aren't just a transactional way to relate to God. You don't give words that are so directive they violate people's authority to make personal choices. This is how many cult leaders became cult leaders: they injected themselves in between someone and God, and took away that person's authority to choose.

God has always given us free will, and the Bible endorses our will to choose. I am always trying to give words in an inclusive and submissive way. Somebody might respond to a word I give by saying, "No, that doesn't make sense or apply to me." And I would say, "Okay." I wouldn't feel rejected personally just because that person rejected my spiritual perspective.

People seem to treat spiritual perspective and prophecy either with contempt or with too much reverence, idolizing it for the wrong reasons. They think people who prophesy are gurus who can solve their problems. But God promises us through the Word that if we make Him our leader and follow Him, we'll experience the greatest possible quality of relationship with Him and with the world. This has to come from having a secure identity in Him, so it's not just a voice in our head telling us what to do. It's the nature of God leading us.

Imagine if you were married to someone who was controlling and took away your choices. That would not be a fun or healthy marriage! You need a partner, a person who adds value to your life, a person who will serve you as you serve him or her. God isn't looking for servanthood based in performance. "You are mine, so you have to do such and such." He has always expressed that He wants relationships that are based on love, with people who freely give their lives to partnering with Him. Having strengthening relationships and a healthy vision for our relationships is paramount!

I did not end up getting married until later in life—and it was *right on time*. I was in the church and in ministry for many years, and lots of people prophesied over me about who I would marry. You may think this was great, but it was actually really frustrating because the words would contradict each other.

Sometimes I would have to interrupt people who were prophesying and tell them to stop. One woman told me I was going to marry someone with a history of prostitution and daddy issues, someone really broken I would have to help. But I had spent years working on understanding myself and my identity and my relational process, and I said, "That will never happen. Identity is attracted to identity, and I would not be attracted to that kind of woman—unless she was taking responsibility for her healing and she was on a journey toward maturity that I didn't have to instigate or manage." I was able to push back on that word because I knew I had freedom to make choices in line with my convictions.

Christ died to give us freedom to choose. We choose to become mature in our identity that the Bible pictures as His bride. He chose to be our bridegroom because He values us. He could have made a different choice; He made that choice from a place of freedom.

How much does this tell us about how God wants us to be empowered to make our own choices in life? I would say a lot. God is not controlling, and He doesn't want us to feel as if we made choices based only on what He or someone else said. If we did, they wouldn't be *our own* choices.

When I step back and think about people's simple desire for God to tell them who to marry, I start to understand that they are often looking for a leader and not a father. A good father never wants to pick their children's mates for them; a good father wants to raise them to be powerful individuals who can pick spouses based on the goodness and identity they perceive in them. A father wants his child to bring someone into the family who upgrades and delights the whole family. (If a father does arrange a marriage, it wouldn't be based on love, but on necessity or tradition. I think most people in the world share my belief that arranged marriages are often destructive and that God intended marriage to be based on love.)

Now place this as a guiding principle for whenever we hear from God: He doesn't just want to meet our spiritual needs by giving us a directive word. He wants to change us, form us, and transform us. He wants to create abundant life in us, which allows us to make powerful choices. Hearing God through others becomes a support to what God is already doing in us instead of defining us externally.

Now, of course, God can speak to us about anything, including who to marry, but my point here is that God is in the business of creating substance in our lives and purpose in our days—which we choose with Him. Many people pursue words about marriage or money out of fear, selfishness, and desperation, not out of emotional or spiritual health, or a strong identity. While God wants the desperate and weary to come to Him, He isn't always going to give the answers we want to hear. We must keep in mind the big picture of what He is working to accomplish in our lives.

GOD GIVES REVELATION TO EMPOWER, NOT TO CONTROL

I think part of the reason we want God to give us these words of direction is that we hope they will allow us to skip over the real and sometimes hard processes of building a life. We want to inherit something without building something, because building takes time. For example, the process of relationship building can be painful or tedious. We'd like for something significant in the future to be so spiritually destined that it will be perfect and make us happy.

In other words, if God tells me flat out who to marry, that person has the potential to solve all my brokenness and relational problems, and I can bypass having to look at myself and work on myself. But God created the process of developing maturity, and He calls it good. I believe one of the purposes God has for marriage is helping us see weak areas and nudging us to grow relationally. If God wanted everything handled spiritually, He never would have come in the flesh for a relationship with us. He would have just transported us into our eternal calling as perfect beings, and we would have served Him without agenda. But that would be like God having artificial intelligence and calling it His children. His plan is so much better.

God is looking at you as your Father, saying, "I love to give you options out of my favor for you, and I love to see what you'll choose." He doesn't always speak about the things you want Him to speak about, because He is showing that He trusts you. He loves you and entrusts you with so much responsibility, and when He speaks, it is to encourage you and empower you in what He has already put inside of you.

Some of us don't realize we're that awesome to God. Some of us are waiting for God to come on a recovery and rescue mission. But think beyond the problems and the anxiety you are experiencing—imagine those were fixed. Then what would you want or need God to talk to you about? Wouldn't it be about how to steward your good life, because you already felt rescued from the Enemy?

God loves it when you decide what you want to do, because He's a good God. He has put inside of you desires that are from Him, and He loves when you identify them and act on them. Isn't that amazing?

As a father, when I see my daughter make good choices, I come alive. As a Father, when God sees you do awesome things because your heart desires what His heart desires, He is delighted. Maybe you say to Him, "Oh, Dad, can we talk to that person walking down the street? I have so much compassion for her." He will always be responsive to that. He'd reply, "Yeah, I love that! You are hearing *My heart*, and I have been waiting for you to want to partner with My love. I was not going to force you to do anything, but now you are choosing to share in My desires and love." God sees us making time in our lives for things that are precious to Him without His having to say it. It reveals a higher quality of relationship, showing that we know Him and can initiate His love in the world.

All that being said, there are times when prophecies will give life direction. Sometimes God shows us things to help love and encourage people toward important decisions in their lives. There are times of revelation that may seem to bypass this relational process I am describing because Jesus is our Savior and will help us out of bad choices we have made. After that rescue, though, God has created in us the ability to thrive.

When you have made the investment of going after partnership with God, you are not a victim to this world any longer and you are not living out of fear for the Enemy who comes to kill, steal, and destroy; you are looking for God to add life and life abundantly (John 10:10). You know when God is showing up in a tangible way, it's just God adding His blessing, favor, and abundance to what He has already built inside of you and what you are already partnering in.

BECOMING WHO WE ARE SUPPOSED TO BE IN RELATIONSHIPS

I knew one woman in her late thirties pursuing ministry, and there was a time period when, every few weeks, someone had a dream, revelation, or word about marriage in her near future. She really wanted to be married, but she had given up trying to find the right person. These words helped her have hope and motivated her to put herself in places where she could meet a man. Without the words, she might have hidden behind her disappointment and not continued to try. It's hard to keep trying when you feel like you keep failing.

Because she stayed available in her heart and ready, she did end up meeting someone and got married a few years ago, well after the prophetic words would have taken place if their time frames were accurate, but they were still helpful. The fulfillment was happening now that she was engaged in the process of marriage. Everyone was happy for her, and the relationship was so fulfilling.

She now can look back and say that those words were the bridge of encouragement she needed to get there. But the relationship was not based on the words alone; the words just encouraged her to get there. People wanted to see her married because they loved her and were praying into it and sometimes speaking into it with time frames, details, and encouragement that were from good hearts but were not always accurate. She had to just stay steady in her identity, knowing that she was ready if someone came who would be a good partner regardless of the words.

The words were not her leader, but they did encourage her. If she had taken them directly, it could have created a wrong leading voice in her heart over her marriage journey, where she would fall victim to the wrong time frames and become disappointed with the lack of fulfillment. Instead she became the best version of herself and practiced the love of patience.

There are other times when God shows us His love for a person or situation to confirm, restore, and empower him or her to have a better relationship. This can be so encouraging to our hearts. I once was at a conference when God gave me a word that was a mystery to me. I didn't understand it (which is often the case; it will take participation from another person to release the impact of the word). I saw 2 Peter 1:4, a verse that says we are called to "participate in the divine nature, having escaped the corruption in the world caused by evil desires."

I saw it tied to one particular woman and told her, "I see 2 Peter 1:4. I am seeing that and thinking second Peter is the one for you. Does that mean anything to you?" At that point I thought this made no sense and half expected her to look confused.

But she replied, "Oh my gosh," and started weeping. It turned out that her first husband's name was Peter, and her second husband's name was also Peter. The second Peter had been bringing her the divine nature—the love and affection of Christ—the whole time they'd been married. Her first husband had been a wonderful man. As a matter of fact, the two Peters had been best friends before the first Peter died. She married the second Peter about fourteen years before this moment at the conference. Only God would know how to say that word so it made sense to her and connect with her so deeply about being remarried and in love after already experiencing the love of her life in her first marriage.

These are the types of things that God speaks into—unresolved issues in our hearts, which we aren't in touch with every day—and brings about healing or closure. Only God's love knows the interior of our hearts and can speak into their deepest places.

The kind of vulnerability we reach after ten therapy sessions can be reached instantaneously when we can see through God's eyes. I love therapy, and I recommend it to just about everyone, because it can really help you learn about yourself and your relational process. But when we hear God, sometimes it helps us realign our hearts so we can have a better relationship with someone or with ourselves. Hearing God helps us give others more grace and be more empowering in areas of weakness, whether others' or our own.

God is part of your inner dialogue. He is your teammate. His desire is to nurture you and help you navigate life so that you can have successful relationships. He does not want to be alone in His work; if He did, He would have stuck with only creating the world and the animals and never created Adam and Eve. He never would have asked them to participate in stewarding the earth. He chose to create you, and He is already at work creating a good life for you. You just have to be willing to participate in that work. Reading the Bible, applying it to your life, and keeping a thriving connection to the Holy Spirit will cause you to change completely from the inside out.

PARTICIPATING WITH GOD TO BUILD A NEW RELATIONSHIP

My friend Rachel was deeply wounded by a few relationships and endured a lot of trauma growing up. When she was a teenager, she asked God if she was ever going to get married. She wasn't sure she wanted to. After she asked, Rachel saw in her mind, in the same way she could imagine a piece of art, a picture of herself next to a man. She saw his height, his build, the way he carried himself and spoke. She saw that it was a healthy, wonderful relationship.

While Rachel continued to tell people she would never want to get married, that picture had been seared into her mind and would come up every time she said so. As the years passed, she started to date, but nothing too serious. Rachel spent years working on herself, received help from therapists, and developed high standards for a relationship. She was in a really healthy place when she felt God asking her to start dating and be open to initiating a relationship. She figured if God asked, maybe she would learn something good or important, whatever happened. Or it might just help her move forward in another step of her journey of personal and relational growth, so she did it.

Later that week Rachel met and started to date someone, a godly man named Tyler who was a good fit for her in many ways. But she was still not a very trusting person. Echoes of mistrust started to resound in her. One of the memories that replayed in her head was of a close family member who had been kidnapped by a man she was close to. He sexually assaulted her, and she was barely able to escape with her life. Rachel was uncomfortable dating someone who, despite having a great reputation, still felt like a stranger.

But one day she came home and, as she was walking over the threshold of her house, that beautiful picture she received as a teenager, which had not been on her mind for so long, rose up in her spirit. Rachel realized the man in that picture was Tyler, the man she was now dating! God had given her a vision that helped her cross over her threshold of fear and have courage.

Suddenly, Rachel was empowered to consider moving forward in this new relationship because God had spoken to her eleven years earlier. God is outside of time, so even though Rachel and Tyler had the freedom to choose who they wanted to be with, He knew they would choose each other. He went outside of time to tell Rachel that it would be a good relationship eleven years before it even happened. Even though she put in a lot of work herself, the confirmation that picture gave her helped her let go of a lot of fear.

Rachel did not turn off her relational knowledge and skills or try to avoid the relational process, which means it still took time to get to know Tyler and build a relationship with him. She also did not stop looking for confirmation that he was the person she wanted, because she knew God always gave her that choice. But she integrated her own information with the information from God, and it kept her moving forward.

Rachel also asked God about Tyler. God's heart is for us to have good relationships, and He took good care of her heart in the process. He told her things about Tyler and shared His love for him. Seeing that built her bond with him. Through borrowing God's view, Rachel saw someone who was honest, trustworthy, loyal, kind, empowering, not controlling, loving, and generous, someone who would do anything in his power to make a relationship successful. She had never heard God endorse someone like that before, and it was not something that would be in her own mind. It gave her a greater context as she continued to grow the relationship.

Because she was so wounded, Rachel had a long list of triggers and artificial red flags that could have easily caused her relationship with Tyler to end. But God told her about some of the things that might trigger her before they happened. She still had serious struggles a few times, but the man was kind, helpful, and supportive, which helped build their connection. She also took responsibility for those triggers and realized that they took away from the fullness of what the relationship had to offer. She worked hard with God and supportive people to make herself "trigger-proof" with her partner by always believing the best, even when it felt scary.

God used the prophetic in Rachel and Tyler's journey to build trust and connection by also speaking to Tyler. One day he was praying for her, and God gave him a word of knowledge about her address and her middle name, which she had never told him. This could have creeped her out. (It might have creeped out anyone with or without past trauma.) But because she knew God spoke this way, it confirmed the relationship for her. It was impossible for him to know these things about her!

Well, Tyler might have been able to find her middle name online, but he could never find her address. At the time Rachel was renting a room in a house with six girlfriends; it was a temporary situation while she was working in that neighborhood. No one in her life had that address—not her parents, her best friends, or the DMV. She had another primary residence, so she'd never had mail delivered there. She'd never signed a contract, and the only people who knew she rented a room there were the people in that house, who had never heard of Tyler. In fact, when Tyler asked her if that was the address, Rachel said she couldn't even remember the address because she had never used it. She had to go outside and check to see if it was the same address!

Eventually Rachel and Tyler did get married, and today they have a thriving relationship and are doing astounding things for God. God helped them start on a firm foundation of health and His love. He guided them in building a relationship through His words and through a natural relational process.

So, God does speak about relationships. In fact, He is speaking all the time about them, but sometimes it's not as directly as we would like. God wants to speak to us in ways that empower us to have the best relationships possible—with our families, our friends, our acquaintances, everyone we encounter. But we can't forget that building and improving those relationships requires our full participation with Him.

THE PURPOSE OF THE PROPHETIC

The thing God wants others to come to know most through the prophetic is what His love is like. That is it! He shows His love through this gift. I find it so exciting to operate in the prophetic because anything can happen. But prophecy with love as its goal never becomes a circus; there's order to it. It is a place where mysteries can be revealed and where we can see God truly knows and loves people. To me, there is nothing more profound than that.

The purpose of the prophetic is to show that there is a relationship available to us that is greater than we've ever imagined, one that is possible only because of Jesus Christ. If we do not value relationship and the relational process, we actually miss out on the good life Jesus died to give us!

We find God in the *process* of things. He's in the process of relationship building and business building. Some people want to use a word to get a quick fix or get rescued, but He actually won't rescue people who can't sustain the rescue. He might do it once for them, but He's not going to do it continually. He wants to use a word to give them an opportunity for greater love. When we lose sight of that, our desires and the things we think we need can easily become destructive.

God let people walk around the wilderness for forty years because He loved the process of transformation He could bring them into. He wouldn't give them something they would never thrive in doing, or something that would actually destroy them, just because they asked for it.

God would rather give you a word that reveals His nature more than one that meets your immediate need or desire. He would rather give you a word that will prompt you to work to learn the skills of how to be love, give love, and better understand love. He'd rather *change you* through a process. He's that good. And He created us for love and relationship—it is our ultimate destiny!

I hope you've seen in this chapter that the ability to have healthy relationships is the key to being able to see through the eyes of love. You must be willing to partner with God in your own personal growth and in establishing good relationships with everyone you encounter and prophesy over.

If you are wondering where to start in loving others through the prophetic, I would recommend thinking about the top twenty-five people in your life and asking God about all the things He loves about them. Ask about His plans for them, His design in them, and the talents He has given them. Carry the prophetic perspective about how good they are in your heart. Then tell them about that perspective, or offer just natural encouragement—whatever you feel about them and what God must feel. Tell them how beautiful they are! Tell them how wonderful they look. Notice the things that they take extra care to nurture, the things they are passionate about, the things that make them come alive. Encourage them about the things they spend their time doing. Encourage them about their relationships, how they live and love as a mother, a father, a grandparent, a son, or a daughter. After twenty-five times you'll feel what it's like to encourage people in a deep way, and you'll start to be able to apply that spiritually.

4

PROPHECY IN
PERSONAL IDENTITY

I was born with a disability. My tongue was tied, and it caused me to be unable to say certain words properly, especially words involving the letter *r*. I had to have surgery, which helped immensely (although I still can't say *rural*). When I did begin speaking more properly, I was very loud, and that continued until I hit puberty. Often one of my family members would say, "I can't wait until your voice changes!"

Then one day my voice did change. Literally, in one day, I sounded different. One of the girls in my choir said, "You sound exactly like a frog!" Although the teacher told her it was a rude thing to say, the damage had been done. Hearing comments like that one, plus years of not liking the way I sounded to others, made me feel unqualified for performance or public speaking.

Yet that's exactly what I began doing over and over when I was a young adult. I started taking platforms to face tens of thousands each year, and I always had this nagging voice in my head that I had never articulated to anyone: *I wish they had someone else to speak to them who is more pleasant to listen to and more gifted as a speaker. But I guess God chose me, a weak person, to show He is strong.*

Can you imagine how that must have made God the Father and Creator feel? I know how I feel when my daughters believe even a small lie about themselves. I do everything in my ability to disempower it for them. God is way better than I am! I love how He solved my problem.

I was at an event and found out that a radio promoter, who placed DJs on the radio all over the Midwest, was there. I didn't want to be a DJ but loved hosting and presenting, and I was super embarrassed to speak in front of him.

"What is going on with you?" my teammate asked me. "I have never seen this kind of insecurity in you! Your courage normally inspires me."

"I don't want that radio promoter to hear my voice," I answered. My heart was filled with anxiety.

My friend looked at me in disbelief. "What!" She laughed, but with compassion.

I told her all about my background with voice troubles.

"I never knew! Our entire team thinks you have a fantastic voice and that you shine whenever you speak."

I felt so stupid—first of all, for telling her. Second, for having the insecurity. And third, for being at the event. Then I got called up to the stage.

My passion for Jesus and people took over at that point, and it turned out to be an amazing night.

Afterward the radio promoter came up to me and said, "Young man, you have one of the smoothest voices I have heard, and if you didn't have a call to ministry, I would recruit you for our main station right now! As someone who has a gift from God to hear people, let me tell you what God has shown me: you were made to be heard, and you have the perfect voice for your calling."

Right then and there something deep within me broke. A lie that had sat in my heart and had blocked me from enjoying myself and my calling was gone. Shattered.

I asked my friend if she had put him up to this. She laughed and said, "No way! It was God!"

THE IMPORTANCE OF KNOWING WHO YOU TRULY ARE

God is the One who knows you best. He is your Creator, and you are His masterpiece. He has hidden all kinds of value in you that you get to discover for eternity. God is also your Father, and He is lovingly nurturing you into having a full belief of who you are. He knows your true identity and who He created you to be.

When you have a revelation of this, it changes your whole life. Until you know your true identity, relationships are hard, scary, and not as fulfilling as they are meant to be. You will have obstacles blocking you from connecting with the Father and connecting others to the Father. Living in your true identity is how you gain true power to step into God's calling for your life.

Our identities are attacked from the time we're young.

Throughout the years we get misdirected by messages from other people, media, and culture, and become confused by hurtful experiences. Until we're back in touch with the original design God has for our lives, there will be something else filling that place, and it will always be something destructive.

So many issues we have are identity issues, rooted in some kind of disconnection to self. One of the deepest of these is self-hatred. For religiously motivated people, self-hatred is sometimes masked as righteousness or piety, because we are denying ourselves—even if it is the self that Jesus died for.

There are people I've prayed over who have been delivered from self-hatred. I've seen cutters stop cutting. I've seen people who struggled with suicide for years get a love for life; I've seen people who say they touched a realm of heaven, and it made them say, "Why did I ever want to die? I'm awesome!"

When you touch heaven and see through the eyes of love, you want to be like God and you want to be the real you. You become grateful that He created you.

When I read the Bible, I relate to Jesus' self-proclaimed favorite disciple, John. I think I am His favorite. You should feel that way too! I also think I'm my parents' favorite child, and it's sad for my sisters. It's just sad.

Just kidding!

My point, though, is that I *feel* my parents' love. I have received and internalized it, and I live with these beliefs: I am enough, they do not want anyone else besides me, no one could replace me, and I am fully loved.

This is such a big issue in the world, including the Christian community. It can determine whether or not you can see through God's eyes, because if you can't have healthy self-love, which comes from knowing His value of you, then you can't love your neighbor as yourself. And if you don't have a strong sense of identity, it's hard to speak God's words to others because you can be swayed easily.

There have been times when I have prophesied next to people who had much more life experience than me. They knew how to interact with God about way deeper subjects. They had better theology. They had better understanding. And I was just me. But I was comfortable in my own identity and simply going after the heart of God. I had to realize I was more than my gift. If all I could do was be an encourager, I would just be an encourager. I naturally tell people what I like about them, because I love to enjoy and celebrate people. And that's one of the keys to starting in the prophetic—to be a celebrator.

To be effective in the world, we have to know that we are well-loved children of God and that He takes great pleasure in who we are. He is well pleased with you!

PERFORMANCE FOR OTHERS VERSUS INTIMACY WITH GOD

In our current world culture, including in many of our churches, we are not loved for who we are. We are loved for what we do. This starts when we are young. If we get good grades, if we listen to adults, if we have great talent, we are loved!

There have been many entertainers, politicians, and actors who have told me that before they were famous, no one cared about them. They had no good friends, or their families weren't supportive. Then they were recognized for their gifts and began living in fear because they knew in their hearts that without their gifts, no one would care about them, not about their true selves. So they live with masks.

Many of them drink, starve themselves, or get involved in pornography or promiscuous behavior because they feel invisible. They'll take on these destructive behaviors because they're so desperate for more fulfilling identities. But these identities based on the wrong things end up destroying them; they are not rooted and grounded in love.

Growing up in the church, I saw many people focus on performance—and then deal with a lot of failure and disappointment. They put more hope in what they could do than in who God was. Their identities were based entirely on what they could do, not on *who they were.*

The truth is, you will never be effective if you think of yourself as simply a culmination of what you do. You are so much more than that!

If you've grown up with a lot of emphasis on performance, it can be hard not to see that as who you are. Unfortunately a lot of spiritual gifts, including prophecy, are used in a way to support this wrong emphasis, to tell people how they can become more useful to the church or their families. These are nice things, but if a person prophesying doesn't have a strong and healthy identity, he or she can perpetuate an unhealthy culture and stay in a never-ending loop of performance-based prophecy.

"Do this, and that will happen."

"You are called to serve here."

"God has made you to be in this role."

These kinds of prophecies can be either helpful or damaging depending on who is prophesying. But I think people experience an identity shift when they're dealing with the true prophetic. When they prophesy over people from love, they start to see how good the Father is, which can override lies they have believed about religious performance.

If you've struggled with living with the wrong emphasis on performance, let me call you to something deeper: focusing on developing true intimacy with God.

My way of moving away from a performance focus was actually hearing God for people—not from a place of being a prophet, but from a place of friendship with the Lord. He began showing me, "This is how much I love them, and this is what they've been through." It happened especially when I traveled to some of the most conflicted places in the world. When He allowed me to connect with how much He loved people who are homeless, in red-light districts, or in high conflict areas, He showed me who they truly were, and then I could see how good He was, regardless of their circumstances.

There was a time when I ministered to men in a maximum security prison who would never be released and have a normal life again, and I could see how the Father treasured them. They could never do anything that would be considered significant in society again—participating in family life, or changing the world through ministry or business. They were stuck in jail, paying for their crimes. And yet I could feel God's full love and complete value for them.

For me, religious performance broke off when I finally reached the point of asking myself, *What am I working so hard for? He's given His grace so freely!* Then I went through a deeper swing into a love-based approach to life, where there was rest. That was one of my favorite experiences.

THE HOLY SPIRIT IS YOUR
IDENTITY COACH

I am going to share stories in this chapter about people who came into their true identities through hearing God, just as I did in the story I shared about my voice struggles. These powerful stories may not apply to you directly, but they may help you answer these soul-seeking questions: Do I have a healthy identity? Are there new aspects about myself that the Holy Spirit wants to teach me?

It's not possible to develop a healthy identity—your true identity in God, apart from any performance—if you don't have a relationship with the Holy Spirit and if you don't have deeply grounded relationships. I'm talking about real relationships that don't revolve around ministry, a job, or a particular role; relationships that aren't based on what you accomplish with others. I know people who go to churches and are only as strong in their characters as their performance in their churches. When they leave that setting to serve somewhere else, their characters suddenly fall apart, because their previous churches were the container for their "healthy characters," which were actually performance identities. I think this is why many people have spiritual midlife crises. They are driven by performance only, and eventually they get disillusioned and disappointed with doing stuff for people, for family, for significance, even for God.

Having a relationship with God through His Spirit gives us an opportunity to grow in intimacy with Him. As we are tested through the trials of life, either we will live from the strength of that intimacy with God, or we will crumble because we can no longer handle the negativity of what it feels like simply to perform.

74

My friend Blake was in ministry since he was a teen. He started preaching at age eighteen and was hugely successful, but it began to feel empty when he was invited to share stages with some of the greatest leaders in Christianity. There wasn't a ladder to climb anymore, and there wasn't a way to measure his performance or impact. It was all a blur.

Then Blake heard the voice of God ask him, "Do you want to walk with Me?"

Blake thought he'd been doing that; he was one of the most successful ministers in his stream. But he'd run out of zeal and hope.

Of course Blake answered yes, and he made a transition into a walk with the Holy Spirit and the Father's love.

He now has a much more narrow focus and a smaller reach, but he has made a more visible impact and has watched God's love transform lives. To get there, he had to go through a spiritual detox, and that made him into the man he is today. God radically changed his inward life, which changed his external life and everything he is doing in ministry.

When he first started prophesying, Blake would use the prophetic to gain influence. After about eight years of that, it left him feeling unknown, burned out, and even disillusioned with the prophetic. He wanted to quit ministry altogether. And that might be something important to hear. Some of us actually think, *Having an extraordinary gift will make me happy or fulfilled.* But it won't if you're not happy with God right where you are now, apart from any gift. There is something else that you need, and it's not position. As a significant spiritual leader, Blake was not happy or fulfilled; he wasn't sure of his worth and sonship and identity.

One day, when he was just beginning to walk more closely with the Holy Spirit, Blake requested prayer from someone, hoping to partner with God in a solution for his struggles. As the person prayed for him, Blake fell into a trance, and God started to speak to him. He began to realize just how oppressed he was. He realized the Holy Spirit was the gift that connected him to the Father, and that his focus on the work of ministry had led him away from the Father and away from grace. He had been trying really, really hard to gain the approval he already had!

Blake then began ministering from a heart of affection for Jesus instead of a drive to perform for Jesus. In a way, he'd already known about this important distinction, but he realized in a deeper way that ministry was supposed to be about healthy relationship and partnership and should feel fun and enjoyable. Blake stopped caring about the results and instead focused on working to reveal that God is not distant or detached from our lives, that He is a loving Father who wants to unlock the best in His creation.

Blake said something really profound to me: "Most people are not asking if God exists. They are asking if He cares and how much He cares. They are wondering what difference His care could make in their daily lives."

Blake said it comes down to belief systems; we live according to what we believe, whether consciously or unconsciously. We need the help of our wonderful Counselor, the Holy Spirit, and people we trust, to help us see that. He even went so far as to invite his friends into his situation and ask for their help and support when he was being critical of himself. Blake spent about eight months not reading the Bible, because he was in a pattern of letting Bible reading drive him to focus on performance. He also took a break from books on preaching or speaking that were helping him develop his skill set. Blake instead spent that time just with the Holy Spirit, asking to learn how good our Father is. To be a son was to be loved, no matter what, and to have full access to the goodness of God at all times.

Another revelation Blake had was that if we are not secure in our identities, we will be afraid of punishment and afraid of loss. But with the Holy Spirit forming our identities, being wrong does not have to crush us; it can help us cling to Him. All the punishment Blake felt he could ever deserve from getting a prophetic word wrong or losing an opportunity was what Jesus took on the cross to redeem. He finally received God's love for him and accepted himself as God did, and Blake is now giving this love to others from a deep, true part of his heart. He knows it, feels it, and is thoroughly convinced of it.

GOD LOVES US AS WE ARE

When we know God sees us and loves us as we are, it changes everything. We don't operate out of fear in our relationships because we are secure.

At a youth camp one night, I began prophesying and said to one of the young men, "God doesn't care what you're not doing. He actually doesn't even care about the things you think you're doing wrong as much as who He says you are." And I gave him a list of facts about him, including his name, his mom's name, his dad's name, and his birthday, along with more revelation and words of knowledge.

Later, at the end of the youth camp, he gave his testimony in front of everyone and said, "I have been struggling with something for three years, and I thought if God ever talked to me, He would just want to call me out on that thing and tell me how wrong I am. I didn't want to come here because I heard there was a prophetic man coming, and I knew if God spoke to him about me, I would get embarrassed.

"Then that man gave me a message from God in front of all of you. God never mentioned that thing. He mentioned what He loves about me. And it made it so easy to break a sinful pattern in my life because I want to love Him and protect my relationship with Him at all costs."

The kindness of God's love leads us out of things that would destroy that love, and this young man experienced that through one prophetic word. He saw love.

GOD REASSURES US OF HIS LOVE

There was a time I was speaking in front of a group of major evangelical and music world leaders, and it was challenging to stand firm in my identity in God's love. I felt such a strong pull to perform through my message and prophecies. I wanted to be profound, but no awe-inspiring revelation or inspiration was coming. I knew many of these people I was speaking to could outperform me. But I also knew if I tried to impress anyone or go into performance mode, it would actually take away any spiritual power God wanted to bring.

As all these people were looking at me, waiting to hear some profound prophetic message or spiritual truth, I kept looking at a lady in the back and hearing over and over from the Holy Spirit, "Tell her 'God loves you.'" That's the only word I had.

I thought, *I can't say that.* I was prophesying around a bunch of people who were capable of so much more than that, and I felt I needed to bring my A game. *Really, God? Are You going to give me more if I say that You love her? Is this a test? Is there going to be more? Please?*

And He didn't respond, because His love *is* His A game.

So I had to make a choice. I could give nothing, or I could make something up—which many people do. I could use prophetic jargon to sound awesome but not really give a word. Or I could give the word God had given me, which was the simplest word.

Then I thought, *I'm really not a performance guy. This isn't about how good I look or how impressive my words are. I just want to see people loved by God. So, if that's the only word I get, I'm going to tell her.*

I pointed at the lady who was in the back row and said, "Hey, you, the lady back there."

She didn't respond.

It felt so awkward for her as I told her, "No, the lady wearing the red sweater and the gold hoop earrings. Yeah, you."

She looked like a deer in the headlights, obviously mortified.

"I just have to tell you one thing," I said. "God really loves you."

The woman, who I'll call Marie, literally fell out of her chair screaming and crying. I had no idea what had happened. No clue. It turned out that she had been depressed and driving around aimlessly, trying to figure out how to end her life.

In front of the whole crowd, Marie said, "I told God, 'I don't know if there is anything left to live for. I don't know if I'm ever gonna do anything good in my life. I don't even know if I believe there's a God.'"

Marie hadn't been to church since she was a little girl. As she'd been driving she'd seen a church, a bunch of people around it, and someone opening the door. Then she'd had a strong impulse to go inside to where we were. She'd said, "I'm going in there. God, if You're real, talk to me and tell me that I'm worth it. Tell me whether I have any value at all. Tell me that You love me. And if You don't, I'll know You're not real and there's nothing worth living for."

I learned that night that obedience to the simplicity of love is always worth it. Sometimes you don't get to see the fruit or hear the positive result, but I thank God I got to that night when Marie fell out of her chair and caused a huge scene. I was so overwhelmed and kept thinking, *Thank You, Jesus! She needed to be loved by You!* And I was so glad I hadn't changed the word or tried to perform. The simple word I had to offer met her need perfectly.

That night Jesus invited Marie to follow Him, and she accepted. She gave her life fully to God and began allowing Him to be her Father. It was beautiful.

GOD'S LOVE BREAKS THROUGH BONDAGE AND REDEFINES US

Identity is a major issue, regardless of where you come from or what your life may look like to everyone else. My friend I'll call Megan came from what most people would consider a good, privileged home: her family was financially well-off, her parents were still married, her siblings got along, and they were Christians who went to church twice a week. She was smart and academically several grades ahead of other kids her age. She was a very hard worker, had won awards in sports, and was a nationally ranked athlete. Her coach was banking on her to be their next champion, which was a big honor. As a young child Megan had dedicated about fifteen hours a week to her sport, and then it became like a full-time job when she got older. From the outside she was living a great life with a bright future, and everything looked spectacular.

But Megan had learned to work hard with people without learning to connect well, and no one really knew that her core identity was deeply broken. Inside, she felt sure she was a bad person, but she could never figure out why she felt that was true. As she entered her teen years, Megan was self-harming, on and off depression medication, and in therapy for an eating disorder and depression. Meanwhile, she was still performing at a high level in school and sports, but she kept her focus on performing as a way to escape her pain and emptiness.

By the age of sixteen, Megan was tired, worn-out, and without any sense of her true identity at all. She never cried and rarely laughed or smiled, because she didn't know what made her sad or happy. She was annoyed whenever people mentioned God because she didn't believe in Him. She hated Christians, finding them obnoxious, fake, and oblivious to reality. Her family was upset with her because they thought she was being difficult on purpose, out of a desire to be mean or spiteful.

Megan did not believe in love; she thought anything that seemed like love was actually manipulation. What a hard place to be in. How can people help you, and how can love transform you, if you think love is nothing more than manipulation?

What no one knew at the time was that Megan had been

sexually abused by more than one person in her childhood and on into her teen years. Abuse of any kind can shatter an identity and one's ability to relate well with and feel connected to others. That is what it did to her.

To make it worse, one of the abusers was a Christian in a leadership position, and another was someone she had looked up to most of her life, someone she had loved and deeply trusted. Like many victims, Megan had developed a core identity formed around self-blame, hatred, and shame of what others had done, and she kept trying to cover the pain and anger by overperforming in school and in sports. It finally got to the point that her false sense of identity was actually destroying her.

Megan felt she couldn't trust any of her therapists because two of the people she'd loved and trusted with her inner world had hurt her the most. She no longer trusted anyone enough to share what she really thought, for fear it would lead to her being a victim again. Because of what she had been through, Megan became stuck in a place where she felt it was impossible to get help without abuse. Not long after turning seventeen, she had been fighting an internal identity battle for four years, and she felt that her life was a waste.

Megan had no idea what to do next and no motivation to figure it out. Lacking the energy to perform any longer and feeling she was beyond the point of being helped, she became more depressed and unstable. Eventually she had to drop out of school and sports. She spent hours staring at the walls in her room and felt as if her heart was dead.

One day, out of absolute desperation, she decided to go to a church around the corner from her house. She often saw people standing outside this church, and they didn't look like the people at the church she grew up in. These people didn't seem to care about appearances and performances. They had tattoos and wore street clothes to church. It was at this church that Megan had an encounter with God.

She went into the worship service in a dark room with loud music and started to feel the presence of God. At first she was terrified. She ran out of the building and planned on never coming back. But she did desperately want help. So Megan went back and started asking God why He was showing up now and where He had been. What had He been doing with His time that was so important that He couldn't have protected her or seen how much pain she'd been living in every day? She felt as if God were standing twenty feet in front of her with His back turned, not caring that she even existed, as she yelled out her pain to Him.

Words came into Megan's mind that she would never think on her own. God spoke to her, saying, "I'm not over there. I'm right here." And a picture came into her head of God with His arms wrapped around her, being close with her, even in all her pain and the terrible experiences she'd had. He was comforting her.

She started weeping. Megan knew this love was not self-seeking, abusive, or manipulative. And that really is part of the power of the love of God. God has zero need for us and never benefits from using us to try to fulfill some agenda He has for His own gain. God already has everything! There is nothing for Him to gain in this world apart from relationship with us. That is part of why we are so valuable to Him. Our performance does not impress Him; it's not what He wants. All He really wants from us is the one thing He gave us control over giving Him: relationship.

From that day on, a new identity started to be formed in

Megan around the power and truth of God's love. She felt it was the only good thing she had in life, so she began to devote herself to it, spending eight to sixteen hours every day praying, worshiping, and attending church. She started to embrace the identity of someone who was loved, someone God thought was worth spending time with.

Eventually, God put it on her heart to talk to a pastor who she'd heard speak several times at the church. Megan tried to say no, but He kept pushing her forward. She was very shy at that point and hated men; she would never initiate conversations with them if she could help it. Megan remembers struggling to hold even a second of eye contact with this pastor as she said she thought she needed help and that God wanted her to talk to him, and that she didn't know what else to say.

This pastor started to prophesy over Megan about her true identity. He offered God's love, shared God's hope, and said that she would go further in ministry and helping others than he had. (At the time, he was running a ministry reaching up to a thousand teens per week.) Megan was shocked to hear him say she would help other people; at that point she knew she couldn't even help herself without God. And isn't that the truth for all of us? Most of us just don't get to the point where we're forced to realize it so early in life—that without God's love, our best performance moments are not enough even to help ourselves.

This pastor said Megan was good, not bad, and that she was meant to live empowered but needed to take responsibility for that.

This is a key part that is often left out of transformational stories, and I want to highlight it because it comes back to the topic of process. We sometimes want to think the ending to this kind of story is, "God said that perfect thing, and then she lived happily ever after." But the reality was that Megan was so bound up in the victim mentality that she had to work hard to change, actively partnering with God's revelation to separate herself from that identity.

The victim mentality is part of the carnal nature, which chooses to reject God as savior. It is not from God, so it cannot save us, restore us, or empower us to move toward a good future. It is an inferior identity that is at war with our identity in Christ. One leads to death and despair (as Megan knew well), and the other to abundant life. She couldn't live as a victim and have abundant life.

Megan chose to be absolutely abandoned to God, and six months later, she was a totally different person. No depression, no self-harm, no eating disorder, and an invitation to prophesy with some of the pastors from the church as they traveled. Therapists would say this was impossible, but impossible things can happen when you live with access to the wonderful Counselor 24–7.

Megan started attending a school of ministry, then she started leading and teaching, and eventually she became involved in and leading outreaches. She ministered to others who were broken and suffering with depression and self-harm. She has had a rock-solid identity built on an experience of knowing God as the only safe thing in her world. Megan allowed God to teach her about her true identity and cocreated that new identity with God from nothing. That identity has caused her to be not only emotionally stable but emotionally thriving for many years.

Megan returned to a high-achieving way of life, but now it is an expression of her healthy identity, not an attempt to fill her lack of identity. She not only has achieved a lot in her life but also has learned how to connect with others. She became a leader in her family, helping them to have healthy relationships and identities themselves. Love transformed Megan, and she now lives as a new creation, birthed from pure love!

We don't have to come from something really broken in order to have problems with our identities. We don't have to come from abuse or depression to need to be transformed to understand and embrace God's love in new and deeper ways—or for the first time. If we don't have the same sort of bondage Megan had, we often have some other kind of bondage.

Regardless of our pasts, I think all of us end up coming to a place of needing to find more of our identity in Christ. And in that way, our stories are all more similar than different. Until we experience God and His heart, we won't be able to move forward in power. Eventually we will be unable to withstand the pressure of our bondage, and something will end up causing us to hurt people unintentionally.

It's a difficult process to begin to reshape your mind by unpacking those areas in which you might be trying to gain God's (or your own) approval. This is why we need to hear from God, because He gives us much greater options than we would have apart from our connection to Him.

Though these stories may look different, they represent all our stories in one way or another. The common theme is that love gives us our truest identity. Love wants us to feel whole and connected to others. Love wants us to feel that we have a strong and sure identity in our Father God. And God wants to speak to us about our identity and what He sees when He looks at us: people who are completely and totally lovable.

5

PROPHECY
IN MARRIAGE
AND FAMILY

When we see true love, it moves us. Why are so many blockbuster movies romantic comedies? Because love stirs something inside of us like nothing else does.

God is Love, and love looks like something. Apart from Jesus, there is nothing that shows off God's personhood, nature, and reality more than a healthy marriage and a connected family.

God loves marriage and family—it was His idea first! They are containers for demonstrating the character of God's love, which is why family is something God is always talking about. It is one of the main areas that the prophetic comes to breathe into.

The Holy Spirit is always there to disciple us in our relational and character choices toward love.

GOD LOVES OUR CHILDREN MORE THAN WE DO

My friend Lisa Bevere once described how her oldest child, Addison, always commandeered all the toys in their home, and her second son, Austin, would have to advocate for ownership of his favorite items. On his fourth birthday Austin received a Lego motorcycle and was so excited. Lisa explained to him that it was his and only his. He was filled with pride whenever he played with it.

One day, when Lisa finally had a few free minutes to take a shower, Austin ran into her bathroom crying and said, "I've lost it! My Lego motorcycle is gone!" She told him where to look for it, but he still couldn't find it.

The Holy Spirit told Lisa, "Tell him to get on his knees and ask Me, and I will show him where it is."

No way! Lisa thought. *I don't want him to get disappointed in God if he can't find a toy.* She later described this as a "mom fail moment."

Now even more distressed and desperate, Austin came back in the bathroom crying, and Lisa relented to the Holy Spirit.

She instructed her four-year-old, "Honey, ask Jesus. Get down on your knees and ask Him."

He sincerely did, and you know what? He heard God's voice

for the first time. He ran to the other room, then returned to Lisa, holding the toy. At that point he couldn't care less about the toy; he was so impacted by the fact that God loved him enough to help him find his toy.

That boy is now in his twenties and still remembers how much God cares for him because of that experience, which was foundational for everything else God did in his life.

What Lisa realized from the experience was that God the Father loves her kids more than she does and that He wants to engage them.

GOD COUNSELS US ABOUT
HOW TO LOVE WELL

Since families are the proving ground and container for God's love, they are a top priority for God to speak into. But we often don't expect they are, because we don't think creatively about what to have faith for. How do we listen to God about one another and about our futures? How do we see one another the way God sees us?

My friend Jim told me about the time his son Ian came into his home office, sat next to him, and said, "Dad, I want to be a singer."

Jim was a little shocked, because Ian had never chosen music even as an elective, and now he was talking about it as if it would be his career. Ian excelled in sports and math, but Jim had never seen him be creative like two of his other children. He was about to discourage Ian, then thought, *I'd better pray and get God's perspective first, before I try and redirect this, because I might be shutting something down.*

It turned out that Ian was an excellent singer, and he went

on to sing in a well-known traveling band. Jim almost missed his opportunity to father him. Instead, he chose to be a part of his son's inner journey, not just because he encouraged him in his music, but because he was sensitive to seeing Ian through God's eyes and not his own. We are always making judgments based on what we can see on the outside, but God sees the heart.

I once invited Katy Perry's parents to come minister at my church, and I was so taken by their love. Keith, her father, shared how he went through a period of disappointment in Katy because she wasn't living the life he wanted her to live and even represented opposing values. He started to back away from her in his heart.

But the Holy Spirit said to Keith, "I want you to love your little girl no matter what. If you give up your fathering role and your love for her because you disagree with her, she will find a father somewhere else, and I guarantee you that person will not have the right agenda for her. Love her!"

It was so impactful for Keith that he and his wife, Mary, found a way to be close with Katy and fully support her, even through career choices that would normally disconnect relationships because of differing value systems. They put up boundaries without sacrificing love. At times that can feel like walking on a tightrope, but love has really good balance! Love can help us walk through the most difficult places.

HEARING FROM GOD FOR THOSE YOU LOVE

Sometimes we are hopeful that if we could just hear from God for the people we love, we could solve their problems. We want to bring solutions and help and grace for the complications of life. That can be one of the goals of the prophetic, but it is subordinate to the greatest goals: to build relationship and to advance love.

Romans 8:35 tells us that nothing can separate us from the love of God—not "trouble or hardship or persecution or famine or nakedness or danger or sword." It's not just poetic; it's what God is building. He brings us a love that nothing can penetrate and that covers a multitude of pains.

When you hear from God for those you love, it's first to build more of that love between them and God. It's wonderful when they receive a revelation from the people they value most, because it makes them feel more connected to God's revelation. Second, it brings more connection between you and them, because you see them with more affection.

When a close family members experienced a huge betrayal in one of her most important relationships, she was devastated and inconsolable. None of us could encourage her as she isolated herself. I lived states away from her at the time, and she wouldn't return my calls.

Then one night I felt God say, "Her heart is open right now. Remind her who she is!"

I didn't have a prophetic word to tell her, and even if I had, she probably wouldn't have received it. So I just texted her about who she was as a person and the value I saw in her.

She called me right away, crying and laughing, and said she had opened her Bible that night and asked God to heal her. She hadn't been expecting anything, but she'd heard Him clearly reinforce her identity. She'd told Him, "I don't feel this is true, even if it once was."

It was in the next moment that she received my text, which

repeated exactly what God had just said to her. And finally she felt that she was able to break out of a rock, a place where she'd been stuck.

God said to her, "I am giving you a soft heart for the stony one You have given me."

And she was back to her old self again.

When someone is family to you and you have history with him or her, you speak from a place of authority. It's the result of love. We should expect that this is one of the greatest authorities God wants to use.

THE POWER OF THE
MARRIAGE RELATIONSHIP

There is something profound that happens when you open yourself to marriage, and your heart can take in what your spouse says in a unique way. It's as powerful as your own internal convictions when they speak truth or lies to you. In the same way, your spouse can be your best personal prophet and affirmer of truth because of their access to your heart. It is one of the most empowering relationships you can engage in. There is nothing like looking into the eyes of your spouse and seeing their faith in you when you're about to take a giant risk or important step in life.

If you want to learn to grow in seeing through love's eyes, use the holy relationship of marriage as your proving ground.

When I was preparing to work on my book *Translating God*, I felt I was supposed to write a love-based, theological approach to hearing God's voice, an approach that would transform readers' understanding of the prophetic. I love seeing God's love transform our culture, helping us to become the best versions of ourselves. I wanted to speak on engaging culture and impacting creative arts.

But I was conflicted. I wasn't sure about writing on that subject at that time, because I didn't want to get typecast as a spiritual charismatic who only talks about hearing God's voice. And I didn't want to step into the public center of prophetic culture, which in my mind was a specialized market that consisted of mostly older people, many of whom are of a very different Christian culture than I am.

My wife, Cherie, challenged me and said, "You are a reformer. You are called to help people hear God's voice. You are called to normalize relationship with God and demystify the prophetic. You don't have to be branded by all the things that have gone wrong with prophets and charismatic ministries. You can rebrand prophecy with love, at least in our sphere of authority."

I was filled with courage.

If someone else, even a prophet I respected, had told me that, it wouldn't have meant as much. But my life partner, who walks with me every day, could make a special kind of impact. She had the confidence to speak faith into the weak place of my heart and build me up.

I didn't know *Translating God* would eventually become an international bestseller, or that it would inspire people all over the world to have faith in prophecy. I wouldn't have guessed that it would lead to other bestsellers, a popular podcast (*Exploring the Prophetic*), and a rise from twenty-five thousand engagements on social media per week to about a million. I never would've dreamed that God would use the subject of hearing His voice to be the catalyst for any of that!

My wife did a very significant work with God when she gave

me the courage to look at myself as a reformer. Cherie helped me understand that the prophetic isn't a niche gift but one of the main expressions of God's love and power in the Bible.

Love's eyes help us to see the potential in others. Why *wouldn't* we see revelation for the ones we love the most when we love them with God's love?

A MARRIAGE THAT ALMOST ENDED

Disconnection in marriage happens all the time for all kinds of people. Some live as glorified roommates or workmates for their families; others just fall out of connection and love. People constantly make bad choices to do life alone again, and that is why we have a huge divorce rate in our society.

The good news is that Jesus said, "I came that they may have life, and have it abundantly" (John 10:10 NASB). That means having abundant life in our marriages too.

A ministry couple I know (we'll call them Ryan and Tameka) are both very strong individuals. Sadly, they went through a silent and hard separation. No one saw it coming—not even Ryan and Tameka.

"For years we hadn't even dated each other or been intimate," Tameka said. "I think we used each other for relational needs, but we hadn't looked into each other's eyes in so long."

"I just threw myself into ministry and being a father," Ryan said. "We were so busy, and I figured the relationship would just work itself out when it needed to."

Then Tameka caught Ryan on his phone with pornography, and it was a tornado in their marriage.

"I knew he was not getting his needs met through me anymore, but I didn't know he'd turned to something else," she said. "I was avoiding conflict."

"I didn't even feel sexy to her anymore, so I just avoided sex," Ryan said. "I had gained forty pounds and didn't feel attractive. I turned on porn. She got mad and began a separation process based on that and on how far apart we were."

This is the point in the story when I came into the picture. After Ryan shared with me that they were separating, I sat down with him and asked if he would pray with me. "Let's do some listening prayer," I suggested.

We sat across from each other, and I said we were going to ask God a series of questions and expect some answers. I prompted him to start with, "God, what do You love about my wife?"

As we sat there, Ryan thought of all kinds of things. He complained that he didn't know if it was God answering, or just things he knew coming to mind, but I said, "Let's keep going."

Then I had him ask, "God, show me the love You have for me to give to Tameka."

He was blocked here and couldn't hear a response. He felt shame and anger, so he couldn't hear God in this area.

Next I suggested he ask, "In what ways does Tameka show Your love to our children and friends?"

Ryan had a lot to say about her here. He was very impressed with her mothering and her friendships.

We kept asking these kinds of questions, and he had so many memories come up and encouraging things to say.

Then finally I had Ryan ask, "Is Tameka the wife You want me to have?" It was kind of a stupid theological question (they were already married), but I wanted him to have to answer it again in his current season.

Ryan knew she was. He just knew it with everything in him. There was no divorce in his heart anymore. He had to win Tameka back. He didn't know if she would want him, but he wanted her.

I helped them connect with a therapist so they could get healthy again, and I set him up with a life coach so he could learn how to live in his passions again.

One year later Ryan and Tameka were dating, going on weekend getaways (which they called their sexcations), partnering at church together, and leading a Loving on Purpose course for married people.

Fast-forward six years beyond that, and they couldn't remember what not being in love was like. And all this started with Ryan's asking God for revelation on who Tameka was. It started with his asking what God's love looked like for her.

God has solutions to our marriage crises, and sometimes when we see His solutions, it gives us different options than what we would pick out of responsibility (even religious responsibility). God always brings things back to relational value.

A FIFTH CHILD WHO WAS ALMOST ABORTED

A strong Christian couple I know had four children, and raising kids had been the hardest yet most rewarding experience of their lives. When the couple we'll call Greg and Julie were finally at a manageable stage in their family life, they found out she was pregnant again (even though conception shouldn't have been a possibility for them). They didn't believe in abortion, but the thought of bringing a child into their already challenging lives felt like more than they could bear. They found themselves actually considering abortion.

Julie opened up to one of her close friends, and that friend said, "Call Shawn Bolz." And they did.

We met the following day, and they told me their story. They'd had a lot of hardships, and I felt sad for them. Then they told me they were considering abortion. Would God count them as murderers? Could He ever forgive them?

"Of course He would forgive you," I answered. "But before you make that kind of choice, are you open to trying something with me? Will you join me in asking God one question, and then wait for five minutes for the answer?"

They said yes.

I prompted them to ask, "Holy Spirit, will You show us who this child inside of Julie is?" They asked it very reluctantly because of their fear, but they asked it anyway.

Greg and Julie were both filled with a vision of this fifth child with their family. It came suddenly and clearly. They met their child through God's heart and revelation. Greg and Julie were instantly in love. They still were exhausted and scared, but they had hit their tipping point—they were going to keep the baby.

I was shocked that God revealed His compassion so quickly. It was stunning. I wasn't trying to manipulate them; I only wanted to guide them in giving God a chance to show them who this child was, and not see him or her as just an object.

Greg and Julie now have a very happy fifth child. Another

beautiful result of their choice was that they were healed from the pain of abortions in their past—abortions they'd had before they were married and before they knew God. God took all the pain away and actively brought forgiveness into their hearts. Forgiveness was no longer just a word but part of their internal belief system.

As we navigate a world full of difficulties, our families can be either one of our greatest obstacles or one of our greatest benefits. We need to hear from God about the people in our families. When we do, He will give our families abundance, health, strength, and joy.

6

PROPHECY IN LIFE DIRECTION

God's love is powerful. Through it we can get prophetic words, which can entirely redirect our lives. Encounters with God help us get in touch with our God-given identities, and our lives naturally change directions as a result. And sometimes when we are simply walking with God through regular seasons of life, we sense that following His plan means making a massive life change. In this chapter we will explore further how God leads us and helps us make transitions in our lives.

Hearing from God is a relational process, not just a random gift that forces us to stay plugged in to communication with Him. We get a revelation about a transition we need to make, we take the steps, and then we need more revelation and continued access to God's heart and thoughts to take the next step.

I've never met someone in a life transition who wouldn't love to receive more wisdom or discernment. A lot of people hear God enough to make the transition, but they don't stay plugged in to their intimacy with Him enough to stay the full course and find out where God is leading them. They don't know that He's not just leading us to a destination; He's leading us to the fulfillment of His promises to us.

DELIVERANCE AND REDIRECTION IN AN INSTANT

I once was at a meeting in a church where a lot of broken people attended. Prostitutes often came, only because someone invited them—they'd never been to church or hadn't been in a long time. One woman who was attending regularly said she didn't know why she kept coming.

One woman we'll call Kim came up to me and said, "My boyfriend is a drug addict. I've been living with him. He beats me all the time." She was bruised all over. She began to cry and tremble. "I just want to know if God's love is real."

Now, I'm just a normal guy. I don't know how to respond to these things any better than anyone else. But in that moment, I related to God, and I started to feel that I was hearing God's heart for her. The words just flowed out of me.

"Do you have a secret bank account?" I asked.

"Yes."

"How much money is in that?"

Kim told me the number, and it was a decent amount of money saved up, in the thousands.

"I want you to go to the bank and empty that account. Then go home and give it all to your boyfriend."

"How dare you!" she snapped at me. "That is the worst advice. I would never do that!" She became extremely angry with me. Kim had come to me hoping to have a moment that would reveal God's love was real, and instead I told her to give away everything she had to her abuser. She looked at me like I was the worst minister she'd ever encountered, the worst person in the world.

Just when Kim was about to storm off, I said, "Well, you're already giving yourself to him, and you're worth a lot more than a few thousand dollars."

Sometimes God gives us words that don't make sense to our natural minds but are meant to help people react and think in a healthier way about the direction they should go with their lives. I never would have thought of this on my own, but with God's help, it came to my mind.

It was the exact thing Kim needed to hear. She went through complete deliverance in a second. And she was done with him.

She went home, along with some people from the conference. Together they packed up her stuff, and she moved out.

How could Kim do this so abruptly? Because the culture of heaven literally gives you value and makes you feel like the original design of God. And when it does, it changes the direction of your life so that it's lined up with the designs He has for you.

OPENING DOORS WE NEVER KNEW WERE THERE

The prophetic opens up doors to help people see through the eyes of love the direction God has for them and to live life more abundantly. It helps them get in touch with whatever it is they need to work out to get there. When people see what's available to them, they can change.

When I was at a homeless shelter years ago, I looked at a Southern white guy and felt the Lord say to me, "If you'll bring him home and let him live with you as he goes through rehab, I will change his life. I'm going to make him a father. Right now he's just a boy in his head." And he was older than I was at the time.

God, that's a huge risk.

I hadn't even had a conversation with this man yet, but I began to prophesy over him. I told him about being a father and not just a son, and that broke him, because he felt he'd never be a father after the decisions he'd made. He'd become a drug addict in college, then he'd been on the streets and on meth for eighteen years. He'd done some pretty terrible things.

But I told him, "God can recreate your full destiny. And you have a sense of what your destiny is because you went to college to play sports before drugs ruined your life. God sees that self-image problem that developed when you were in college, and He wants to heal it. If you'll go after God right now, He'll heal you and recreate your whole destiny."

This is a marvelous mystery of God's, and I have seen it unfold time and time again. God is so good that, even if we spend eighteen years missing His will, we can still get back on track and live out the fullness of what He has for our lives with whatever time we have left.

God is not bound by our earthly time, which is why some people can get delivered in a second. In their hearts He has done ten years of work in a second. As God works outside of this world's linear time, He can take what a person's past should have been and allow him or her to live in the fullness of that in the present. I have seen this happen time and time again.

God will allow some people to connect with Him in a way that helps them fulfill in five years what most people would achieve in twenty-five years. He can make it so that some people can have a better relationship with Him after five years than others walking with Him for twenty-five years. For me, it's one of the most incredible mysteries to watch play out. God has expedited processes He wants to provide for us so that we can be empowered to change the world and fulfill the purposes He has planned for our lives.

The homeless man began to cry. He hugged me and said, "I never thought God could recreate a destiny."

Yes, our God can recreate your destiny, making it as if it were new again. And you'll have a place of significance and thrive in life, even in relationships. Even if you've done terrible things and wasted all your life, you can still have a full, redeemed life in God on the earth.

Did you know Christians are the only people who believe that? People from other religions don't believe their god recreates a destiny. How hard it must be for them, because they don't have hope! Even if we're living with the results of bad choices and brokenness, we can always have hope that God will enable us to live in fullness, in a freedom that can be felt even when physically imprisoned. Whatever our circumstances are, God can give us a place of significance in our relationship with Him and the people we're around.

FEELING GOD LOVES US
THROUGH DIRECTION

God brings new life direction to people all the time, and sometimes it comes in the moments they least expect it.

I was once on a plane, feeling grumpy because I don't really like airports, and I started a conversation with someone sitting next to me, who we'll call Joe. He told me how excited he was to retire in two weeks. Normally, I don't share specifically what I do, because people think I'm crazy, or they want me to solve their problems, or they feel that I'm judging them. But I did tell this man I was a Christian speaker who taught people to hear the voice of God.

As the flight continued, I began to hear God speak to me about Joe—the directional change God had for him, how much God loved him, and what he wants to do. I also heard God tell me, "He's the air marshal."

Now, this was a hard situation, because I didn't know how Joe would react, and I still had to sit next to him for the rest of the flight.

I told Joe, "Hey, remember when I said I am a Christian speaker and I help people hear the voice of God? This might sound weird, but I feel that God has put some things on my heart to share with you."

"Okay," he said. He seemed fine with it.

"Well, I'm going to start out with your family." I told him things about his daughter, that she was an advocate and a political science major. I had some words of knowledge about her pursuit of justice causes and about her marriage. She and her husband had almost broken their engagement over some conflicting justice issues in their hearts, but they chose love. They chose the highest road. Joe had spoken into their lives to help them through that, among other things. I gave him a framework of what had been happening in his family, what God saw, and how God had been helping his family all along the way, even when they hadn't known it.

"But what you don't know for your life as you retire is that God is going to give you the power of justice," I said. "The same drive that's in your daughter is in you. And it's going to be the power to advocate against a major-cause issue. I think that cause is human trafficking."

Tears came into Joe's eyes. "I want to start an anti–human trafficking organization when I retire."

Joe didn't spend time interfacing with folks who do this kind of thing all the time. In his world, he's the only one who cares about human trafficking. I understood this and wanted to add the last piece about his current job. Because he had tears in his eyes. And because I wanted him to know without a doubt that he'd heard a directional change in his life, and it was all from God.

"It's God who has put this in you," I said. "And to prove it all, that this is really God, I want to tell you that God knows you're the air marshal."

"No, I'm not," Joe said adamantly. "I'm not the air marshal. Everything else is true, but I'm not the air marshal."

"You're the air marshal. I know you are." I felt so sure about it.

Joe just kept saying, "No. I'm not. No, I'm not. No, I'm not. Shut up. Don't say anything else. Don't talk."

We had seven more hours on the flight, during which I didn't talk. Joe actually didn't seem angry with me; he looked fearful. When the plane landed, he walked straight up to the pilots before I even unbuckled my belt. I stepped off the plane and walked to the baggage claim.

All of a sudden Joe showed up at the baggage claim and said to me, "I couldn't talk to you while you were on the plane, because I'm not supposed to reveal that I'm the air marshal. If I did, there'd be a security risk.

"I did a background check on you, and I found out all about you. You've done phenomenal things. I *am* the air marshal. On the plane I thought either everything you were saying was from God and that God is real, or that you were someone who was disturbed or messed up or trying to hurt people, and I had to shut you down."

At that moment I was so thankful that I'd heard God and hadn't started the conversation with, "I know you're the air marshal," because then I probably would've been put in jail. Joe probably would've said, "Who are you? What's going on? You must be a terrorist!" I was so glad I got to be part of God reaching this man, giving him encouragement he would never forget, empowering him to transition into the next season of his life, and letting him know God was blessing it.

People want to know about their futures. *Is there hope? Will it get better? Will I become more significant?* God wired us to need hope; it is a resource to fuel our faith. And revelation gives people so much hope! When people hear what God is saying, they become ready to go after whatever is next on their journeys.

I have sat down with all sorts of people who need direction, from billionaires to missionaries to the homeless, and I love when God speaks this way, because making life changes is one of the most complicated processes humans go through. All change can be extremely difficult, and if you don't feel led into it by a caring God, it can be brutal. Thankfully, God loves to comfort and counsel us through transitions and new directions. He also loves to speak encouragement. He is the God of courage!

7

PROPHECY IN RESTORATION

God is in the business of restoration. He restores our hope, our future, our families. Sometimes when we see through His eyes of love, He reveals His original plan for someone or something and will use that revelation to help things shift back toward His perfect design. The story of Jesus is the greatest story of restoration, so it is no surprise that God would make us aware of how this story is playing out in those around us.

God does not want destruction; everything and everyone can be restored. His plan for all people who are in sin and ungodly situations is to restore them to the way He created them to be. The Devil cannot create, so all creation and everything that exists was originally from God and had a divine purpose. The Devil, however, does distort things to try to make them into his own image. The gift of money and financial success can turn into greed. The gift of food can turn into gluttony. The gift of a creative mind can be disturbed by destructive thoughts.

To be agents of restoration in our world, we have to be willing to take the time to pursue God, pray for His perfect will to be done, and ask what we can do. Sometimes we see injustice or something that doesn't line up with the fullness of what God had in mind for a person or situation, and our role is simply to pray. Other times, as we seek His understanding of how restoration should happen, God will reveal a way that we can take restorative action.

RESTORING CHILDREN TO FAMILIES

As some of my friends were praying about an unjust situation and hoping something would change, they began to ask God to interact with them about what they were praying for. A child from one of their church families had gone missing. They'd read in the Bible how God had helped find missing people, so they asked God to show them where this child was.

This led to some clear prophetic pictures of a truck, a license plate number, a description of a man, and more. They began interacting with the FBI and police forces on God's behalf, and their tips led the authorities to find the missing child.

This gave them courage, and they started a missing people prayer team. They said, "Let's develop a team that prays for the missing people in our community and then multiply that around the world."

The head of the team took pictures of missing people from their region and shared them with the prayer ministry and prophetic teams. They all simply looked through love at the plan God had for these people and asked God for details to help restore them to their homes and families. In some cases they would start with a car that was used in a kidnapping, asking about the make, the model, the year, and the color, because it could be helpful to the law enforcement agencies.

They started praying about specific children. Once God gave them a picture of a child and where she was, and three days later, the child was found.

When a local police officer heard the story, he asked them to pray for another missing child. They did, and someone on the team saw a picture with the color of the house, the street address, and the relationship between the child and the abductor. They asked the family about this information, and the family knew someone who fit the description exactly. They found the child in the house from the picture and restored him to his family.

The police department began partnering with this team regularly—enlisting the help of the church to find victims and solve crimes!

The prayer team has created a tried-and-true process: Groups pray for facts and then compare notes. If any of the facts are the same among the group members, they compare facts with a third group to find commonalities. They continue in this vein until many people have prayed into it. Whichever facts are the same for all groups are passed on to the police or shared on a call with an anonymous hotline.

The prayer team is respectful of police and FBI policies and have learned what is needed and how to interact within that system. As a result, they've had success in working with these authorities and helping them do what God has called them to do.

RESTORING RELATIONSHIPS
WITH FAMILY AND GOD

God wants not only to restore people to their families but also to restore their lives to be full lives with faith and love. I once was watching a famous psychic who was not operating in God's plan for her gift, and the parents of a kidnapped girl asked her, "Do you know where our daughter is? She's missing."

"She's dead," the psychic said, "and she was kidnapped by her uncle." Then she told a long story about it with so much conviction that the parents became very distressed.

I ended up meeting the little girl who was supposedly dead. Her name was Sarah, and she was an adult when I met her. She actually had been kidnapped at a grocery store by a stranger and had a terrible life for a couple of years. When the psychic told Sarah's parents that she was dead, they just believed she was gone and didn't look for her anymore.

Then, out of the blue, the FBI found Sarah and brought her home. Her parents were in shock. The whole encounter with the psychic turned out to be very confusing.

When I first met her, Sarah naturally was totally closed to the prophetic. "The prophetic is the reason my parents gave up on me," she told me.

"No," I said, "that psychic is the reason your parents gave up on you. Let's talk about God and who He was in your past." I looked through her life with her and Jesus. I asked her, "Were there any times when God protected you or helped you?"

Sarah gave it some thought and then exclaimed, "Oh my gosh, He was there all the time! I can see Him now. He was so for me. He never left me, even though people abandoned me." She'd had a prophetic revelation that God was the One who brought her out of captivity and led the police to her. Now she was able to stop associating God with the psychic and to forgive her parents.

Many people in the church are not aware that the world needs Christians to help carry out justice. They've given this occupation over entirely to other organizations and religions. Yet the FBI forces I've interacted with are eager to receive support, saying, "We need the cheat sheets from God. We need help." God cares deeply about justice, so we should too.

RESTORING LOST POSSESSIONS

God also wants to restore possessions that have been wrongly taken. My friend David had an incredible experience of finding something that was stolen when he and another pastor friend were ministering in Colombia. One night they had just finished sharing on how God can bring you breakthrough in your finances at a church, and they were heading back home in their car. They stopped at a red light, and a guy with a machete came out of nowhere. David's window was down, and the guy started attacking him. To make things worse, David had all his belongings in a bag in the front seat, including his passport, camera, and wallet.

As his friend covered and protected his own face from the machete, another man reached into the front seat and snatched the bag with all David's valuables. After the guy with the machete stopped attacking David, David tried chasing after the robber, but he couldn't catch him.

David called the cops immediately. They were able to catch the guy with the machete but not the robber with the stolen bag.

It was ironic because David had just been talking about finances and had seen breakthroughs; then he experienced an instant loss by having his own money stolen!

A few days later David was scheduled to leave the country but had to purchase a new passport beforehand. On his way to pay for the passport, the Holy Spirit gave him a vision of the exact address and location of the house where his stolen passport was. He called his friends and asked them to go to that address and look in a certain room, which he saw in the vision. Sure enough, when his friends went to the house and the people living there let them come in, they found his stolen passport!

It seemed as though God was reminding David of His presence and goodness in his life. God saw His child experience an injustice and wanted to bring restoration, which would leave him with a greater sense of how often He protects and spares and redeems. It deepened David's relationship with God and increased his faith that God had his back, always and forever. If God could show Ananias where to find Saul by street name and address (Acts 9:11), He can recover a passport!

RESTORING HUMAN RIGHTS

God wants to restore everything and everyone who is being violated, which certainly includes people groups experiencing racism. There is so much racial tension and prejudices against different people groups throughout the world, and the only way there will ever be a real resolution is if God shows up. God is the ultimate civil rights leader.

I have so much respect for William Seymour, who made

church history and a major contribution to American civil rights back in the early 1900s, when segregation of races was the norm. At the Azusa Street Revival, he brought together Asians and Hispanics and blacks and whites all in one place, allowing them to worship together. He simply heard from God that all people were created equal, that no one should be limited because of race, and then he took action.

Thinking of William Seymour makes me wonder how God might do something about the problem of racism through our lives now.

I know the prophetic is one of the answers. God loves all people—their history, their culture, how they look and talk. Racism is a lie that says God loves one group more than another, or that one group is more important than another because of an exterior or cultural characteristic. It emerges in a belief system where love is no longer the priority. Not to oversimplify this, but the only solution to racism is love—actual, true love—for yourself and who God made you to be, and for others and who God made them to be. It is recognizing the beautiful and unique expression of God in all of us. The Enemy wants to disempower us through racism, which keeps us from walking in our God-given authority.

One of my friends has been dealing with this issue for years and has some really inspiring stories about how God has used the prophetic to help people be restored to love and awareness of how God initially created them to be.

Here is Sean Smith's story in his own words:

Some years back I was involved in a campus ministry, and Tim was one of the students who attended. He played on a baseball team and told me he had a teammate we'll call Jon he'd like me to meet. I was quick to agree. I wanted to meet with any of the students and their friends so I could build a relational connection with them, love on them, and hopefully lead them to Christ.

Tim brought his friend to meet with me when I was standing at a resource table for our ministry at a conference. When Jon walked up to me, I extended my hand to shake his. He stopped and looked at my hand, looked at my face, and then paused for a minute. It got very awkward. I kept my hand reached out to him. Finally he touched my hand and gave it what I call a "limp fish grip." I knew there was something going on with him but couldn't tell what.

The unfortunate thing was that I had to leave right away to keep an appointment. So I said to Jon, "Hey, man, I have an appointment, but here's my address. If Tim will drop you off at my house, I'll give you some lunch."

Now, I didn't know this guy's persuasion. I didn't know that he'd been a junior Klansman and now was a part of the neo-Nazi white supremacists. And here is God's irony. I'm an African American man. There's also some Filipino and Cherokee in me. I've probably got everything this dude would have issues with.

Later, Jon did come to my place, a tiny shack of an old parsonage. One reason he came was that he was very troubled, and another was that he wanted to get Tim off his back. It was as though Jon was telling Tim through his actions, "I want you to leave me alone. My views are my views, and after this, I don't owe you any favors."

At that point I had learned that he was a racist following a neo-Nazi tradition. I wondered what racists ate. Probably not ethnic food. I didn't know what to feed him! I decided on a tuna fish sandwich.

As he had the tuna fish sandwich on his lips, sitting in this little shack with ugly, burnt-orange carpet, Jon looked at me and started the conversation exactly where I didn't expect him to. He said, "I hate black people."

It was at that moment I knew I was saved. If I weren't I would've gotten into a fight with him right then and there. (You can't come over to my house and say, with my tuna fish on your lips, that you hate black people!)

Then Jon said, "I hate Mexicans," and went on to list even more groups he hated.

I stopped him, calling out his name, and said, "Let me ask you a question, man. Why do you hate black people? Why do you hate Mexicans?"

Jon answered, "They took our jobs, they do this affirmative action stuff, they cross our borders . . ." On and on and on.

When he was done, I said to him, "You have no reason to hate anybody else. Can I share with you something that happened to me?" Then I told Jon how my dad had been murdered by a white cop.

For the record, I have great respect for police officers. I have friends and relatives on the police force, and I support them and pray for them. But the particular cop who shot my dad was not godly, had a background in the KKK, and didn't honor his oath. He and his friends cornered my dad one night out at Steven's Creek Boulevard in San Jose. They called him a racial slur before siccing a dog on him and spraying mace in his eyes. Then they chased him down a field and emptied three rounds in his back. My dad was dead on arrival at the hospital.

After telling this to this guy who was trapped in hatred, I said, "You know what? If it weren't weren't for Jesus, I'd have every reason to hate you and your race. But Jesus Christ came in my heart, and He's changed that. And, man, I've got nothing but love for you."

I was just sharing my story, and Jon could have had any response. What happened next was the weirdest thing: he began to weep.

I realize now why God led me to invite Jon into my house. When I first met him at the conference, I could have squeezed in a few minutes with him, but I felt that I heard, "Bring him into your house."

We got down on our knees. Jon kept on crying, and then I began to cry. He asked Jesus Christ to be the Lord of his life.

Jon immediately became my right-hand guy. We witnessed to everything that moved on that campus, and he ended up leading many people to Jesus.

Then something even wilder happened. We came across a black Muslim guy who wore a dashiki and a Malcolm X hat and followed Louis Farrakhan. He was hard core. He didn't even go by the name his mother gave him, which was Deionte; he went by another name. He said, "Man, I hate white people."

"It seems like I've heard this before," I told Jon.

I pulled the black Muslim guy aside. "I'm not going to call you by that name. I'm calling you by the name your mama gave you. You should have a problem with any god who says one pigmentation of people is greater than another pigmentation of people. You hate people and yet you are perpetrating the very thing you hate them for."

"Hey, man, you sold out," Deionte said. "You Uncle Tom." Today he would have said, "You're not woke."

I had just led his fraternity brother to the Lord, and I knew Deionte would be around when I would be discipling his fraternity brother. One day he came to one of our meetings while I was preaching about—of all things!—pride. I started struggling when I saw that dashiki-wearing, Louis Farrakhan–following black Muslim. *God, I don't know if preaching on pride is the evangelistic message for this guy!*

But I felt the Holy Spirit say, "Stick to the script I've given you."

Before I was even finished speaking, Deionte stood up, walked to the altar, and started sobbing. Jon came up and hugged him.

They were both sobbing. Immediately Deionte was no longer a black Muslim. He gave his life to Christ and started going by the name his mama gave him. He became my other right-hand guy. Together we witnessed and led people to the Lord.

One day I was driving the three of us in my car when the Holy Spirit said to me, "Duck in this church." So we stopped and walked inside. It was a church that probably wasn't inclined toward the baptism of the Holy Ghost and the prophetic. I felt led to ask Jon to lay his hands on Deionte and pray for him. When he did, both of them were baptized in the Holy Ghost, praising God in the heavenly language.

I began to see that one of the things that attracts God's outpouring of the Spirit is unity and love among brothers. Then I began to cry as I thought, *My God, we have the answer to racism in America.*

It is the love of God. It is this gospel that reaches far, that knows no boundaries. It is a mercy and grace that comes from the Father above and says, "It doesn't matter what you've done. I'm not going to stop loving you." It's the kind of love that can overwhelm you and give you a surplus of love, so that you can love people who were once your enemies and make them your family.

I started to believe that if we will be like Jesus, we will see our finest hour. Yes, there are a lot of things we have to work through, but it's going to have to begin with having the heart of the Father. God helped me see that when I loved the person in front of me, choosing to let go of any issues I could have had with him, it created a domino effect. He then loved another guy he had reason to reject. Our experience displayed what the love of God can do. What a beautiful, incredible picture! What would happen if tens of thousands of believers would allow the love of God to work in their hearts in the same way and choose to love someone who is not like them?

It is so good when people of different races can worship together on a Sunday. But I think it really gets conquered when we can eat together and break bread together on a weekday night. When you can invite folks who are different from you over to your house and really get to know them, you don't see the barriers you saw before. You begin to see beautiful things in people's hearts and lives. You recognize the decorated image of God.

RESTORING HOPE IN THE MIDST OF DEATH

No matter what is in our past or what issues we struggle with, God is able to restore us. He wants to restore our family relationships when they're broken. He wants to restore our faith, hope, and love when they're lost. One of the most challenging things in life to overcome, and often what shakes our faith the most, is death.

Ultimately, Jesus came to restore us all to eternal life. We were made for eternal life, and part of the pain of death is that it goes against our original design. Sometimes we get stuck in the pain of death for a long time, but God wants to bring us peace and strengthen our faith.

One time when I was speaking at a large conference, a young couple had come there from Texas and had never been to that kind of conference before. I had a word of knowledge for them. I said, "Is there a couple? I think your names are Mark and Frannie."

They responded, letting me know they were present.

I asked about a number that came to mind.

"That's our street address," they answered.

I asked about a name that came to mind.

"That's our street name."

I asked about another name that came to mind.

"That's our daughter."

For a minute we sat in that beautiful experience, where they felt really known by God.

Moving on from that wonderful word, which made them feel alive in God, I offered a really special word to them. I said, "I see your daughter, who passed away at the age of ___, ____ years ago. I see her in heaven with Jesus. I see her praying for your family with Jesus. She's so happy where she is. There's been so much suffering in your hearts because of the things you thought you could've done differently or that you wanted out of this that didn't happen. But she's fully alive, and you no longer have to have your heart on pause. She's a real human still. She didn't go away. She didn't cease to exist. And she's now fully developed."

I began crying, thinking, *Oh, my gosh. If this were my daughter who died and somebody gave me a word that they saw her in heaven, I would be undone for the next two years.*

They'd had such a lack of resolution over this, and something in their hearts was being healed as I was giving the word. Their hearts were being restored to a place of faith and hope and peace. Other people who had lost children were also getting healed in their hearts.

"You can take her stuff that's in the closet and under your desk that you haven't been able to part with and release it, because you don't need that now," I told them. "You have her in heaven, and you will have eternity with her."

They cried hard, and later I did the same because I just love how God wants to restore our hearts. He wants to raise our hearts from the pain of death that we were never supposed to experience in the world He originally created.

This is the power of God: there is nothing that is lost that cannot be restored in some way. Maybe not immediately or in the time frame we'd like, but how much worse would it be if we were stuck in a world where things could not be restored through God? Where we couldn't be relationally restored to God because of sin? Where the people we love were not able to be reunited with us, either now through a word about a kidnapped child, or in eternity through the power of God?

Jesus was called to bring the restoration of all things. That means this is one of His main passions. Whenever there is anything that is undone in your life, your family, your society, or the world, you can guarantee that God is commissioning heaven to address it—that He was watching and moving well before you even saw it.

Jesus didn't get victory just over death and life; He also got the victory to restore the Father's original design and purpose for all things. If we can see that desire and hear His heart, then we can help bridge the gap by faith and bring restoration the whole world is waiting for.

8

PROPHECY IN
ENTERTAINMENT

The entertainment industry affects most of our lives and our children's lives more than any other industry, even more than education. The average household in America or the Western world spends about six hours a day engaging with social media, television, or video games. On top of that, children are usually more receptive to the interactive experiences of video games and the visual images of media than they are to verbal and visual teaching in schools. In fact, the average child spends only about seven to ten minutes of their attention span learning something in a class before needing a mental break, when they daydream or get distracted.

Love is the catalyst for true change and transformation, so we have to love people in the entertainment industry. This doesn't mean we have to love all that the industry is doing; clearly it does many things that are not aligned with love or with God. But we need to be able to dream and call out the potential it has as well as highlight the ways it is already succeeding by bringing life and hope. God wants us to feel empowered to go impact this land, but He's also occupying this land more than we could ever hope or imagine, and He's about to do something even greater.

At times Christians have been threatened by the vast amount of entertainment that exists and have considered it an enemy. But if we look through the eyes of love, we see an industry that has the potential to impact people for Christ—more than school, and potentially more than the church. God wants to create a conversation with us about what He's doing in the entertainment industry and invite us to participate. The caveat here is that we cannot be given authority to change something if we do not love it first!

We have to watch our thoughts and the things we say in private about those in the entertainment industry. God taught me this lesson one day when I said something negative about a musician. She was very sensual, and I had a negative attitude toward her.

"She's ruining the musical culture in America. I hate what she's doing," I said bitterly to some good friends.

Then God said to me, "I wanted you to meet with her, be a support to her spiritual journey, and speak into her life. But because of your religious bitterness, I can't let you meet with her. You've turned off your love toward her. I have to let someone else meet with her."

It shocked me to hear that! God knows our hearts, and He knows our words have power.

I immediately retracted it. God created that woman, and He

loves her. It hurts Him when I speak negatively about people He loves.

I'm really sorry. Teach me to love as You love!

Even with my repentance I still didn't get to meet with her. I learned my lesson the hard way that time.

The good thing is, when you repent, turn your heart to Jesus, and open your heart to love, you just may get to meet with all kinds of wonderful people God has placed in the entertainment industry. They have great potential to walk out the dream of God for our culture. Yes, we have to speak out against themes of immorality. But our war is not with people; it's with powers and authority structures.

EVERYONE NEEDS CONNECTION TO GOD AND TO LOVE

There's a measure of jaw-dropping things we've seen happen through and with people in the entertainment industry. Most are a lot more open to hearing from God than you might expect. They all have needs and dreams and hopes and disappointments. Even when entertainers are at the top of their game, what is happening behind the scenes is often very different. There is pain and loss, family issues, a constant fear of not getting the next contract, and pressure to be so many things. They struggle just as you and I do, not knowing if they can afford to spend time flying back to visit their family, or if they should say yes to working with someone when they're not sure how it will end up. They may have the same relational poverty that many of us struggle with, and they certainly have the same need to feel loved unconditionally.

Even when celebrities in sports, film, or music know they're embraced by massive audiences for their personas, some still feel that they're failing because their jobs have kept them from tucking their kids into bed for three weeks. They also know they may be loved for their gifts and talent one minute and then scrutinized and ridiculed for mistakes the next.

So the entertainment industry is not full of people who feel that they have it all together and know all the answers. It is full of people who are waiting for you to show up and believe in their greatness—not the greatness of their gifts but as people God created and loves. That is what the prophetic does. There are a lot of people in the entertainment industry who are internally crying out, *I need help!* or *I need answers!* What they need isn't more wisdom; they need connection to God and to people who will love them.

I founded a church called Expression 58 when I realized there weren't a lot of support structures in LA for people who work in the entertainment industry. A good portion of our church felt called to work in the entertainment industry—with the same passion others felt called to be a missionary or to pastor a church. They felt commissioned to see the glory of God outside the church doors.

What if God is planning a transformation for the industry and raising up people in the church to go into that world to shine His light?

FOLLOWING GOD INTO THE ENTERTAINMENT INDUSTRY

When my friend I'll call Sydney was just sixteen years old, God said to her, "I'm sending you into the entertainment industry.

You're going to be an actress." She studied drama and theater at NYU for a couple of years, and after she graduated, she did what actors typically do: she struggled to make ends meet and went to audition after audition. A few doors opened—small doors, but still powerful. She continued to hold on to the word God had given her.

Sydney came to LA for a project and was offered a lot of money to do a show, but it came with a nudity clause. Her agent told her it wasn't a big deal, that she shouldn't worry about it, and she should just sign the contract to get the job. She prayed about it and felt she shouldn't do it, knowing she could lose her credibility by not compromising. But Sydney maintained that no-compromise attitude because she was following Jesus. He lived in her. She could hear His voice. She trusted His leadership.

After not compromising she could have walked away, saying the whole industry was bad, but Sydney didn't. She'd prayed into it and did what she felt was right, trusting God to bring the word to pass.

God started to show Sydney the word *star* wherever she went, and whenever she went to church she kept getting prophetic words that she was an Esther. She learned that the name Esther means star, and this is when God began to impress on her the biblical meaning of a star. Not long after this, someone prophesied to her, saying, "God wants you to go into movies." This person told Sydney that she would be filmed in a particular location. He said that she would meet Oprah Winfrey, which is not a word that comes around very often! That's not like, "I just want to tell you God has good things for you." That's very specific.

Within seven days of that word, Sydney was at dinner

with—you guessed it—Oprah Winfrey. Two months later she had a television show on Oprah's network, and it was filming in the exact place that the person had said!

As Sydney has worked in the industry, doors of influence have opened up for her, and she has been able to impact the entertainment industry with love and the message of a good God. She has become a star in the world's eyes. Sydney believes that God speaks to her directly and through others. In casting meetings, on set, or in life, God is fully capable to impact the world she is in with His love. She believes we need to keep asking God, *How can I partner with You in the manifestation of Your love in this next place?*

Sydney has also paid a price for this. At one point she told her managing agency she was a Christian, and they stopped working with her.

When she moved to LA she had no stability, coming only based on a word from God that she was supposed to be there. Little by little Sydney built her entire career, but not by herself. She partnered with God and with His love for the people in the entertainment industry.

SHOWING GOD'S POWER IN STADIUMS

God also spoke to my a friend we'll call Samuel about getting involved in the world of sports. He showed Samuel how sports can teach kids how to be successful in life, how to have relationships with a team of people, and about Him as well. He began to see a generation of marginalized kids in Canada through the eyes of love. Samuel found a way to empower professional athletes to make a difference in the lives of children. Many professional athletes have a strong faith, but at the beginning of their careers, they usually don't have a platform to reach people. Samuel had the vision to take some well-known athletes who really wanted to help people and host events with them.

I felt that God had stadiums for Samuel, stadiums where he and athletes could host events for kids who were at risk or in urban areas. I gave him the word, and immediately his faith wrapped around it. A specific stadium came into his mind. (I love when I get a word, and a friend feels the word resonate, then God tells him another related detail. It's like supernatural tag teaming—we all work together toward a goal God has set.)

Samuel needed a lot of faith to believe God had this particular stadium for him; it was a half-billion-dollar arena with twenty-two thousand seats. But he just accepted it, saying, "Lord, I thank You for stadiums. I thank You for stadiums." Samuel's process of building belief was based on the principle that "faith comes by hearing, and hearing by the word of God" (Romans 10:17 NKJV). So he spoke it to help himself believe it, until one day he believed it with everything he had.

Samuel started hosting smaller events with a few hundred kids, and before long the crowd grew to more than a thousand kids. When he got an MVP of the NHL to come, more than thirty-five hundred kids, plus more than two thousand parents, attended. Through this experience he saw God work in remarkable ways.

One day a businessman called Samuel and said God had told him to form a strategy to get access to a big stadium. He'd decided the strategy would be to rent the penthouse suite in that stadium for a year so that different people could use it for prayer and worship. The stadium was to be used for God. When the businessman began renting the suite, he invited Samuel to access it too.

Later on while they were in the suite, one of the main players was injured pretty badly as they were watching, and he would have to miss a big part of the season. Samuel's prayer team was using the penthouse suite, and they asked if they could pray for him. He said yes.

Right then and there, God healed him!

A medical team followed up with another look at him and said all signs of the injury had disappeared. All the trainers, players, coaches, and owners had now witnessed the power of God.

It didn't take long until the owner of the arena wanted to know who was behind this healing. He called Samuel and said, "You don't know me, but I go to church twice a year hoping that God will answer one question I have: *Do You have power?*" He said that for the first time in his life, he'd seen the power of God, and he wanted to give Samuel the arena for one day to host any kind of event Samuel chose, *for free.*

It's one thing to think that God wanted to give Samuel a stadium, and another to see the teamwork involved to make it happen. One man with a word from God, one businessman with a strategy, one player who was injured and then healed by God, a large group of people who prayed and worshiped, and a stadium owner—they all came into alignment for the word to become a reality. This is not something that could have happened accidentally!

Thousands of kids came to Samuel's event in the stadium. The stadium owner even promoted it, asking only that Samuel and his team do the same thing in the meeting that they had done for the injured player. Now God is moving in the lives of thousands of kids, opening their hearts to Him, all because He first touched people in the entertainment industry.

LOOKING PAST THE NEGATIVE STIGMA

I wish everyone had this kind of vision to ask God how we can partner with people in entertainment. Sadly, there has been a negative stigma about the industry for a long time. In 1996 people did not have positive reactions when I told them I was called to Los Angeles. When I told Bob Jones, who was an incredible prophet with a staggering track record, that I was moving there, he said, "No, it's not God. Don't go. California is full of sin and will fall into the ocean because God will judge it."

I thought, *Wow, Bob is one of my prophetic heroes, and he can't see any value in the entertainment industry or LA. That is a really harsh word coming from God when I think God is the One who called me.*

But Bob was convinced, and he was one of the most accurate prophetic people I knew. I'd watched him cast demons of cancer out of people; they'd become cancer-free in a second. I'd watched him give words to more than six movements in their early stages, and they all went on to become internationally renowned. This is the man who had helped birth the foundation of faith I stood on. So I figured he was right.

But I also knew I heard from God. Not just a light hearing, like, "You're supposed to go to LA. It's going to be really fun." I heard, "Go to LA and build a bridge between the church and the entertainment industry because I'm going to use popular culture to change culture, and it's going to be a revival catalyst." It was so clear.

Of course I decided to go after it.

I had to tell Bob, "I love you a whole bunch, but I have to reject your word. I don't want to reject *you*. I love you and need you in my life. Even if I'm wrong in this, I'm going to need you on the other side of my move (unless I'm dead from California falling into the sea). I love you, and we're in relationship. I know this will hurt and that it's weird, but I have to reject your word."

Inherent in Bob's word was that Californians had done things that made them unworthy of God's love, and that's just not good theology. In the Old Testament we see that if we disobey, God judges us. In the New Testament we see that Jesus took the judgment on the cross. He became the curse, so God doesn't have to afflict people to get them to learn anymore. He even "causes all things to work together for good to those who love God, to those who are called according to His purpose" (Romans 8:28 NASB). The prophetic in the New Testament is about direct relationship.

Bob was great in his response. He said, "Okay. I love you." And he stayed connected with me.

Bob would go on to warn me about California for another year; he was scared for me. I'd call him, and he'd ask, "How are you doing?" expecting me to tell him things were going terribly. But I was able to tell him how many doors were opening and how much God was doing.

Bob does his best to understand love. He once had an eye-opening vision of going to heaven, and the only thing Jesus asked him was, "Did you learn to love?" This made him realize early on that, even as he was doing ministry, he still didn't know how to love. So Bob knows the power of love. With this in mind I eventually called him out, in an honoring way, about his negativity toward California.

"Bob," I said, "I think it's easy for you to believe the negative words you speak about California with so much passion because it's a place where you've been wounded. A movement that was there hurt your heart, and you've never been able to recover from that. I think you need some healing in your heart before you prophesy about California. You'll never have authority over what you don't love. I think you've missed out on something with California, all because of cynicism stemming from your own pain."

We did an inner healing time. He was completely healed, then he started prophesying for twenty minutes about what God was going to do in California. It was radical.

My response? "This is awesome!"

I tell this story because one of the greatest prophets of love failed to see the entertainment industry with God's eyes. He saw what it wasn't, and he saw the evil it was, but he couldn't see God the Creator anointing creatives all over the world for His purposes. We have to ask God to open the eyes of our hearts to see past our own pain or prejudices to see what He wants.

I also tell this story because it illustrates another key to the prophetic: you need your own relationship with God so you can judge the words you receive and ask God about them. If it's about relationship, and God is the author of a word you receive, then He will confirm it to you. If that doesn't happen, you know it's not from Him, even if the word comes from someone you've never seen get a word wrong.

Had I not been mature with a strong sense of my own

ability to hear God, I would've said, "Okay, Bob. I'm not going to California." And I would have missed the best years of my life. I would have missed my wife. A lot of my friends would have missed their spouses. We would have missed some of the greatest glory stories and experiences I've ever seen—all because I had bowed to fear masked as a prophetic word.

I don't want the church to be known for judgment and fear regarding the entertainment industry. The church is supposed to be known for its love. I want us to look for what God is doing in entertainment and highlight that. We have to recognize that people are on spiritual journeys, and sometimes God has hidden Himself in them. We need to honor that and remember that part of being prophetic is being a friend of God as well as a friend of those God speaks to.

FOCUS ON GOODNESS AND BRING MORE GOODNESS

On this side of the cross, God speaks to everyone. I can't tell you how many world leaders and entertainment folks I've talked with who have had a clear word from God. I was the friend who helped interpret those words, which enabled them to make a huge leap forward in their spiritual journeys. We get to help leaders and influencers know the God who is speaking to them, just as Daniel and Joseph did in their time.

Watching a person create artwork (especially if that person is really good) is one of the most glorious things you can do—just watching creativity multiply, watching it come out of somebody. God first revealed Himself as a Creator, and He loves this aspect of us. We get to see His nature on display in creative people. God wants to reveal His love and heart through entertainment, through people He has called to be athletes, musicians, actors, and entertainers.

God sees people in this industry from the perspective of redemption; they are people He died to redeem. When we refuse to love the people He loves, we inhibit our relationship with God. Most of the people in Hollywood who are engaging in destructive behaviors are doing so because they need the love of God in their lives. They're trying to fill their emptiness and manage their pain with other things. As God's representatives, our response to them should be compassion and love, not fear and judgment.

Some parts of the entertainment industry do so much good. Creative work can raise awareness of important issues, bring joy and distractions from pain, provide a way to rest and relax, and give experiences to bond over. Other parts perpetuate a lot of immorality. But the trajectory of Hollywood can change as we speak God's word. Just as God called Jonah to Ninevah, He wants us to partner with Him to restore Hollywood to a good industry instead of putting it down, prophesying doom, and destroying it. If we don't give words of hope and love, we actually will be the only ones who will miss out. We won't get to see the fullness of what God can do. He has us here to represent Him to the world and take part in His work.

Those in the industry who are listening to God know He has given them the keys to the kingdom, and this is one door they will open wide for the King of glory to come in!

9

PROPHECY IN WORK

We spend a huge part of our lives working, so it certainly should be one of the topics we interact with God about. It was part of God's original design for us to care for and manage the earth, and in eternity we will rule and reign with God. So work is not simply an area of our lives but instead a core part of the kind of beings God created us to be. And if it is a core part of who we are, then God has a plan to help us thrive in everything to do with work and to make a difference in the world of business.

It used to be common for Christians to believe that God's voice is reserved for people doing things that are overtly spiritual and that most things are not to be considered sacred. The reality, however, is that everything God has given us to have authority over and to love is inherently spiritual. You may still come across people who think that not every sphere of life (especially those in which we spend the majority of our time) can have spiritual authority, but that's not true.

God cares about every aspect of our lives, and when we apply this to the business sector, we start to see the moving parts of the kingdom. We start to see how money and influence intersect with kingdom people who are intimate with God, and how God can change the world. What happens when business leaders and their board members ask God for strategies about how to move forward? How to treat people? How to use money to further God's plan on the earth?

God has a design for business, and He constantly speaks about it. People can either turn to Him and move forward in their work through their relationship and connection with Him, or they can toil and struggle without His help, with only their own interests and gain in mind. Business can become a way to reveal stewardship and empowerment in the hands of God.

Every team member in every office can benefit from God's help every day; everyone needs divine strategy. It can happen through one prophetic word. A team may have spent twenty hours and hundreds of thousands of dollars to try to come to a decision, and then a prophetic word can come and create a way that was never even considered before.

THE BIRTHDAY PRESENT

My friend we'll call Addison couldn't figure out what he wanted for his birthday. His friends and family asked him, but he really didn't care this particular year. It was just another day. He wasn't thinking about giving his family and friends the opportunity to be present with him and celebrate him; he was just working hard in a job he didn't love and trying to survive.

Addison was reading portions of Proverbs and Psalms every day, and one of the passages he came across was about wisdom calling out. He felt as though he had no wisdom for what was inside of him. He got employee awards from his current business, and everyone loved his creativity and work ethic, but it wasn't satisfying for him.

Addison asked God, *Will You let wisdom for my life call out to me for my birthday? All I want is Your plan and wisdom for my life. There must be more.*

He pondered this during the next few weeks before his birthday.

On the date of his birthday, Addison clearly heard the voice of God say, "You called out to Me, and now I am sending someone to call you with a new plan."

He was shocked and so excited but didn't know what that would mean.

Later that week Addison received a call from an investor of an entertainment company who had heard about him through a woman at his church. After talking with this woman, the investor had a dream about Addison working for her. She described this dream to Addison and invited him to interview for a position at her company, and he was in shock. It was so exciting and new. He couldn't believe someone who didn't know him had called him and all but offered him a job that he wasn't totally qualified for.

When Addison went to formally interview for her company, everything just fit. He realized this was the type of thing he believed God could do, but something he'd never experienced and had never really expected was possible for him personally.

Now, a decade later, Addison is in God's dream job for him and lives in a place of gratitude, because he surrendered his life to God's plan and implementation.

GOD SPEAKS ABOUT BUSINESS AND OCCUPATION

One of the first promises and prophecies God gave a human was the gift of work to bring Adam satisfaction and significance. If it was one of the first things God spoke about before Adam left the garden, then you'd better believe He is still speaking about it today.

The Holy Spirit is called the Counselor and the Comforter, and these roles are understood now more than ever because we have sports coaches, life coaches, business counselors, career coaches, and mentors. We can imagine inviting or know how to invite someone into our careers. God is the master strategist who created the whole structure of what thriving world markets would look like. He is the One we should be inviting in!

God wants businesses to prosper and His children to live in abundance. He has all kinds of promises in the Bible for His people about prosperity and thriving, and these are not for the sake of just experiencing wealth. The kingdom was meant to function fully resourced, and people have the capacity to live their best quality of life when provided for.

If strategies come from God, they are going to be effective and create change. People will want to work with you and be attracted to your work, even if they don't know why. As Proverbs 18:16 says, "A man's gift makes room for him and brings him before great men" (NASB). When we operate in the power of God, powerful people will be attracted to us. He can connect us with influential people in business and work environments, and they can make decisions that change the course of our culture.

My friend Julian hears God well and is great at coaching people from all types of backgrounds. He began to get invited to meet with some high-powered business owners, though he was not involved in business himself. I joined him in one particular meeting, and we prophesied over everyone there, mostly unsaved business folks.

Max loved these people and had as much authority as I've seen among Christian leaders of the greatest churches; the impact and authority was the same as what pastors and other types of leaders would need.

Max's gift in the prophetic brought him before these "great men" of influence in our world. Everyone, the saved and the unsaved, needs and wants to receive the love of God.

Three people in that meeting heard God's voice for the first time, and Max gracefully led each one of them through that new process. All three of them were saved that day. They received the Lord so beautifully because Max knew how to love well.

GOD PUTS US IN POSITIONS TO OFFER LOVE AND TRUTH

Before I met my wife, Cherie, she and two friends came to a conference I was leading in Arizona. I ended up prophesying to Cherie's best friend, Lauren, saying, "You have the gift of makeup artistry. It's not just a hobby, and it's not just for weddings. You could pursue this as a career, and it would make you happier than anything else."

Lauren had been working as a compensation manager at a casino in Las Vegas, where she was very successful. Her greatest and secret desire, however, was to be a makeup artist in Hollywood. But she wasn't sure how to make it happen logistically and was afraid it would never work out.

Lauren had been around the prophetic before, but this was the first time a secret of her heart had been laid bare. She felt so connected to this desire that within a year she'd quit her job, received training in makeup artistry, and moved to Los Angeles.

After only a matter of months, Lauren became the lead makeup artist on *American Idol* for their Ford car commercials. Ever since then she has been working for one of the best makeup agencies and has had no problem finding work.

I love that Lauren had the foundation in her relationship with God to go on that faith journey based on what was in her heart. She was able to recognize God in it and follow His steps into it. That is something that you only learn through connection to God, when God calls you to a certain career and you know He will open the doors that you have no idea how to pursue directly.

I also love that Lauren's dream was not only to be a makeup artist but also to impact those who were inaccessible to the average person and to love on people in the entertainment industry.

One person in particular Lauren reached was a young woman named Josie who had cancer and wanted to kill herself through assisted suicide. Josie had made national news by saying, "I don't want to go through a degenerative cancer. I want to take my life while I'm still able to function. I want people to remember me this way."

Josie was going to be on the cover of *People* magazine, and

Lauren was assigned to apply her makeup for the photo shoot. Lauren ended up connecting with her in a meaningful, precious way during that time. The details of what happened are between Lauren, Josie, and Jesus, but isn't it encouraging that in these significant moments, when our culture can be impacted, God sends Christians on the scene to love people well? He places them even in positions that may seem unlikely. Josie didn't want to talk to the greatest pastors in the world or a worship leader, but she sure would talk to a makeup artist.

Lauren went from working as a compensation manager to following God into the makeup industry, and now she is speaking truth and love to all kinds of entertainment people. She has spoken key words at the right times to help them, support them, and just be Jesus to them. As a makeup artist Lauren is allowed to talk to the talent while other workers on-site are not. They start to see her as a friend and pour out their hearts to her. They talk about how they're feeling and share their dreams and fears and family problems. They come to trust her, because they feel the safety of God when they talk to her. She gets to love them first, and if God has something to say to them, she is perfectly positioned to give them the wisdom of God for whatever is going on in their lives.

GOD DISRUPTS MORE THAN TECH COMPANIES DO

God wants to infiltrate every area of the world with His wisdom and love. I've come across many accounts of God's speaking and causing crazy shifts to happen in marketplaces and systems. Let me share a few with you.

A group in Southeast Asia has written an early childhood development curriculum based on revelation God gave them, and that curriculum is now being used in several countries. It's now changing education throughout the world, all because they received and followed through on an anointed idea.

Another group has developed a new strategy for helping people immigrate to America and work on farms. With government support, their organization will be hiring hundreds of thousands of immigrants.

A tech group is creating a Bible teaching series involving virtual reality, which will allow people to virtually walk through the Holy Land, creating a new way for them to connect with the stories of the Bible.

Some winemakers received an idea from God about a new invention for distilling red wines. Using their new method the fermentation of fine wine can take half the time previous methods took.

A man who never played with toys received dreams from God about toy inventions. He then created and patented some toys, and the two largest toy companies have begun paying him astronomical royalties based on those patents. He now also leads an inventors' group.

A man self-published what ended up becoming a bestselling book, which made him close to a billionaire.

The stories of what God can do if we just see through His eyes of love and hear His voice for our business world are endless.

My friend Bob Hasson has a service organization that meets the needs of massive companies. (You can read further about his brilliant approach to business in his bestselling book with author Danny Silk entitled *The Business of Honor*.) On one multiyear project with a company, there had been a lot of cost overruns. They went through litigation, and then before things started getting nasty, they went into mediation.

One night during that season, Bob was at home reading 2 Chronicles 20, about when Jehoshaphat was attacked by enemies from all sides. How did Jehoshaphat respond? He went out to his enemies and sang. The enemies turned against each other and killed each other, and then Jehoshaphat and his men went down and plundered.

Bob and his team had an important meeting scheduled for the next day. He spent the rest of that night soaking in worship music to the point where the music overshadowed his voice. He heard the Lord say, "When you get to the meeting, you are not going to say a word."

That seemed strange to Bob because he was the leader and supervisor; normally he talked the most. He didn't understand how this could be a good idea.

Lord, that cannot work. You have missed it this time.

The next morning the team met to prepare for the meeting. Bob shared with his team what the Lord had told him and described what had transpired in his home.

This was all too much information for them; they didn't even know about that part of his life.

But Bob went on. "This is what the Lord said: 'You're not going to speak at this meeting.'"

His team immediately began to question this.

"How are we going to do this?"

"Do you know how important this is?"

"There are millions of dollars on the line!"

Bob was just as confused as they were, and at that point he

was reassured that this had to be from the Lord because it didn't make sense.

They arrived at the job site, walked through a maze of construction trailers, and entered a conference room where there were eight men. For two and a half hours of discussion and negotiation, Bob did not say a word. He couldn't believe it himself.

Finally the lead negotiator for the other side said, "Bob, follow me to my office." So he followed.

Bob sat down and listened to the lead negotiator say, "I'm going to offer you this much money right now." And he wrote down an amount that was not enough. Bob looked down at the man's figure and began to write. He had no clue what he was writing, but he was writing. For all he knew it could have been a message in tongues.

The lead negotiator watched Bob continue to write, then said, "I'm going to raise the offer to this much." And he wrote down an amount that was really high.

Being the good Jewish boy he was, Bob continued to write more "tongues." He figured if it had worked once, it might work again.

Then he finally looked at the man, who said, "You can't argue with me anymore. This is my final offer." Bob simply reached across his desk and shook his hand.

Before he knew it, the deal was done. Bob still hadn't said a word.

Bob and his team walked out of there rejoicing. They thought that maybe Bob shouldn't talk so much after all.

It's amazing how God led Bob in a successful business deal that day. But do you know what is even more amazing? God was reaching and changing Bob's heart through this experience. God wanted to show him that he needed to grow in his knowledge of who he was in Him. He knew Bob struggled with shame and insecurity. It seemed as if God was reminding Bob of who he was and the gifts he'd already received—the ability to negotiate, to mediate, to talk, to understand—and helping him see that the One who gave him these gifts could do above and beyond what he could imagine, if only he'd trust Him.

Something else that deepens the meaning of this story is that when Bob was a teen, God explicitly called him to this kind of work—but not only running a business. When he was eighteen, Bob received a prophetic word that he was going to be a philanthropist. He didn't know what it meant and thought it was something bad, so he got mad at the prophet. Then he asked what it meant, and the prophet said, "A philanthropist is a person who loves to give money." And he prophesied over Bob again about his calling.

Business is just one avenue for sharing God's heart and serving others. Bob does not live in a poverty mind-set in which he must always give all to God. He develops godly strategies for his giving, and he sees himself as a distribution center of time, talent, and money. It's been one of the most phenomenal things for me to watch as God has impacted the world through those resources.

DOING BUSINESS WITH ETERNAL CONSEQUENCES

It is so important to realize that the things we do in our jobs have more than temporary effects. When we work with hearts of love, the things we do have an eternal impact, which is a sobering thought. When all else fades, all that is left will be faith, hope, and love. What will be left from the years you have poured into work?

Gerri, who is on my prophetic team, shared a story from her life that is a beautiful example of how taking a risk can touch someone not just in the moment, but for years and years later, and then even into eternity.

In 2006 Gerri was a teacher, and her assistant principal asked her to begin switching rooms partway through the school day so another teacher could use her room too. At the time she was really upset, because veteran teachers normally got to keep their rooms all day. It was the new teachers who had to "travel" their first few years.

Gerri appealed to the assistant principal, urging him to reconsider, but he would not change her schedule back to staying in her room all day. While she continued to be upset about it, she decided she was going to have to let it go and just give it to the Lord. She knew she could either let herself be bitter about it or be open to this change, helping her grow in some way.

It turned out that the person she'd be sharing the room with was a sweet new teacher, who we'll call Kyra, beginning her career. They got to know each other well as they shared lessons and ideas. Soon, Gerri was looking through love's eyes and was able to see God's heart in it all. Even though it was an inconvenience to move her stuff over to another room every day, it provided the opportunity for her to build this new friendship.

As the end of the semester came, Kyra said she wouldn't be coming back the next year because she'd be serving in the Peace Corps in Tajikistan.

Gerri heard the Lord say, "Take her out to lunch, and buy

her a Bible." She wasn't sure if Kyra even believed in God. But God kept saying it.

So Gerri invited her to lunch, and Kyra said yes. Gerri gave Kyra a Bible with a note she'd written in it, wished her well in her travels, and left it at that.

For a long time Gerri didn't know why God had asked her to do that or if the seed ever bore fruit. Then twelve years later Kyra found Gerri on Facebook and sent her a message. (Even though technology is not all good, I am so thankful for everything God does in and through it.) The message said:

> My husband and I were just doing Bible study this morning, and we used the Bible you gave us before I left for the Peace Corps twelve years ago. What a sweet blessing to read the note you wrote in it, saying that you'd prayed for me and that the Lord had nudged you to give me a Bible. My husband and I have been so blessed to know the Lord and strive to keep Him number one in our lives. I hope you are well! Thank you for that sweet gift long ago.

As Gerri read this, tears came to her eyes at the realization that many times God brings a change into our lives in order to carry out His purposes.

Especially at work, it's easy to despise or ignore what God wants for us when it doesn't look like what we want or expect. But His still, small voice is present in every area of life. God is always speaking and nudging.

All Gerri had to do was turn to Him, listen to His voice, ask Him for the grace to go with the flow and the changes, and continue her walk and work with joy. It became a pleasure for her to meet and collaborate with Kyra, and then it became exciting to see that God had a beautiful purpose in it.

To make it even better, Gerri was given her room back the following semester.

Sometimes all we can see is an inconvenience, but through God's eyes, we can start to see the opportunity and plan that He has. Gerri is so glad she didn't let fear or frustration stop her from blessing someone for more than twelve years!

THINKING OUTSIDE OUR BOXES OF HOW GOD MOVES

A while ago I prophesied over a person who had just switched jobs and was working in sales. I felt that God was going to give this person strategies for his sales, so he would have divine knowledge about who to call and what to say. I also sensed that the success he'd have in sales would be important, because it would provide a financial foundation for a ministry God had put on his heart. What I prophesied ended up happening, and it was the primary strategy this person implemented to meet his goals.

This is yet another example of God moving in a secular arena with a sacred purpose. But the suspicion whether this is the case persists. I see some Christians operate with the assumption that people working in organized Christian ministries are more important than people serving in other roles. This just isn't true, and assuming it is creates a class system among believers. A multinational chairman will not be valued for his participation with the Holy Spirit as much as a pastor of a church is. Christians often don't know how to honor what God has done through someone when it is less obvious than what most people are looking for as spiritual fruit.

God wants to teach us how He sees and help us value what He values. God wants Christians in every kind of job because He created us with talents and skills that we are meant to share with the world, just as Jesus did as a carpenter before He started His official ministry.

You can have a relationship with God at work just as you do at church. It might look a bit different (you're not going to be worshiping loudly all day), but you can still worship in your heart, minister to people you come in contact with, and do your work with excellence, which reflects God. Our jobs are supposed to be part of the divine plans and purposes for our lives. In the garden Adam and Eve worked and stewarded in their given roles. They must have sensed they were living out who they were in a healthy way because it was their divine calling, and they were communing with God and admiring God's creation the whole time.

RESISTING WHAT WE'RE CALLED TO

Sometimes we face obstacles that get in the way of our walking into the careers God has for us. We get so lost or distracted that we can't move forward in our destinies until a part of us is healed and filled with love.

Once I was at a conference and I asked if someone had a son named Mark who was African American. A woman stood up. I asked if Mark had been abused by a corrupt white policeman when he was younger, and she answered yes. He had been stopped for no reason, then pulled out of his car and beaten. I asked if it had happened two more times when Mark was in his twenties, and she answered yes.

It is so painful to endure abuse from people who are supposed to protect us. But God wants to cover the pain with His love, heal us, and empower us, regardless of the bad decisions others have made. He can keep our lives and destinies from not being controlled by those people and their decisions.

I told this woman what Mark's birthday was and that he was born for something great. I asked her to tell him that God said what the police did was totally wrong, that they had misused their authority. God hated that and did not want the actions of these abusive cops to take away Mark's destiny. God saw him as a leader and wanted to use his leadership skills to help define how authority should be. Mark was not stepping into that because he felt lost. His pain was preventing him from living out the fullness that God had for him. God did not want the pain; it was there because people have free will and made choices. But He wanted to use Mark's pain for his good—to motivate and empower him to make a big difference in the world.

The woman gave Mark the word. A month later I got to talk to him and found out that he had applied to the police academy. What I hadn't known when I gave that word, what none of us except Mark had known, was that it had been his secret desire to become a police officer. But after the abuse he'd decided he didn't want to join a broken and corrupt system. The desire hadn't gone away, and he'd continued to feel conflicted and confused. God actually had been calling Mark to be a light in that system, to live out his dream and destiny without fear of that system.

It is beautiful to watch God use the prophetic to bring spiritual resolution. We get to see the root issues keeping people from going into the jobs God has called them to flourish in and the places where He wants to use them to restore justice.

We read in Matthew 4:8–10 that Jesus was tested in the wilderness. When Satan brought Jesus to a high mountain, he showed Him all the kingdoms of the world, tempting Him with leadership of every one. What the Devil was showing Jesus was not limited to religion; it included the businesses, governments, and every role that in some way led or shaped society. Jesus knew that this was what God wanted to restore to His people through His very precious life. He was able to resist the Devil and made a way for us to be coheirs, corulers, and sons and daughters with Him. And then He gave Christians the keys to these very kingdoms. Some Christians are stuck looking only for the growth of organized churches when some of those keys were meant to be used to influence and serve others outside the church, even to take on every role of leadership in society.

God is giving you keys to kingdoms as well. If you can see and love those He loves, He wants to give you authority to bring His dominion and kingdom to them through both servant roles and power roles. Are you willing to take on those roles so others can know His love?

10

PROPHECY IN FINANCES

When we begin to see through love's eyes, we begin to understand how finances are one of the main ways that God helps us become the version of ourselves He dreamed of. Take a minute to think about the nations that are going through the most conflict right now. Now try to imagine what the people who lived in those places could bring to the rest of the world if they were free and resourced. What are their destinies, which are being held back by so much war or pain?

God is a Father and, like any good parent, He wants to resource His children fully so they can be contributors in life. If our Father has a purpose, then He is creating resources for it and has a plan for giving it to us to steward. Many of the parables Jesus used were resource-based because He wanted to give us a stewardship mentality—an understanding that we're called to be resourced and be people who provide resources.

Cherie and I consider the property we currently live in a miracle property. God spoke to us a number of words about this property through others. At one point I thought, *I just don't know if I can believe for that big of a property right now. Maybe that's ten years or twenty years from now.* But we had dozens of prophecies about this property.

On a Thursday in July 2016, I remember hearing the Lord say, "Your property is going to go off the market by Monday. If you don't partner your faith to My word and partner your faith to My heart for you, you're going to miss it."

It was the most generous, gracious thing the Father could have said. Later, after we bought the property, I said to the Lord, *You are a good Father. You could have told me the Tuesday after it was off the market, "I had a house for you, but you didn't have faith." But instead You pursued me!*

Generally speaking, I had faith in my relationship with God, but when it came to resources in certain areas, my faith was weaker. I had to learn that God calls us to receive things that we cannot obtain by our own education, career, or connections. It's hard when He asks us to believe for something like this; it can feel presumptuous, and it can seem delusional to others who don't believe in this sort of relationship with God.

GOD VIEWS MONEY AS A TOOL FOR GREAT THINGS

The average Christian probably doesn't dream with God about world finance, asking what He thinks about it, but we are supposed to care. We are to make His concerns our own, carry out His mission on earth, and become like Him in the process. He is making us into a great reward for Jesus, for the price He paid on the cross. If that's going to happen, we'll need to see Christians stewarding great roles of authority, great resources, great finances, and great influence, because we need the tools, industries, platforms, media, and venues for people to get saved and discipled. " 'For I know the plans I have for you,' declares the LORD, 'plans to prosper you and not to harm you, plans to give you hope and a future' " (Jeremiah 29:11).

I have found that many Christians are actually afraid of money or resources, especially money or resources they can't accumulate through their own efforts. But God does not want us to feel weird about money. He wants us to think reasonably about it without allowing it to be our focus. He wants us to have it but keep it in its proper place in our hearts and minds. I think there are people God has called to impact the world of finance, having put the desire in their spirits, but their minds can't make sense of it because it's such an abused subject wrapped up with warped or convoluted teaching in the modern church.

God wants to provide finances to empower us, His work, and the people in our lives. I see proof of this often. Once while I was speaking, God gave me a word for someone. I said, "Your name is Shray, and you're from India. The Lord says He has given you the heart of an engineer and some sort of design gift, and He's blessing the pursuit of education you came here for. Do you have a master's degree? Was it just a couple of years ago you finished?"

The person named Shray agreed this was all true.

I continued, "The Lord is saying He's going to bless the design gift, that it's going to bring a tree of money. Is there something you work on with money, with software engineering for finance?"

Shray answered that he worked as an engineer with MoneyGrams.

"God will send some people who will mentor you. There's some sort of company that's going to come together with you, and it's going to be great for your family, both for those back in India and those who live here in America. You are going to create purpose that many family members are blessed for, and it's going to create money. It's going to create financing. It's going to create interest.

"I feel that the Lord wants to show you today how much He loves your faith for a better life, for a kingdom life, and how much He loves that you came here out of a belief that He would bless you and your family. I guarantee you that earning a master's degree is taking your whole family to a new level of spiritual and natural breakthrough or a new path has been laid out for your family to come out of broken financial areas. Doing that was an act of intercession that will pay off for generations."

This word I felt impacted not only Shray but his family and church family as well.

HAVING A VISION FOR THE RESOURCES WE STEWARD

Have you ever fallen in love with the people God is calling you to? If you know your mission field, your tribe, who the joy set before you is, then you will need resources to steward this calling. You won't be satisfied if you can't influence them or bring the kingdom to them.

If we have no vision we perish, and the same is true when

handling money. If we have no vision for what God wants to do with our money, we're keeping Him out of a big part of our lives, and we will end up perishing and wondering why God didn't help us. We have to look into His heart and see who He is calling us to love, and then we'll have an expectation that our lives can produce the resources we need.

My friend we'll call Stella was struggling with giving money to her church because she didn't know if she could trust someone to use her hard-earned money well. She was excellent at financial management, and the people who were doing it at her local church were working with small-scale skills, like it was a mom-and-pop shop. When the church leadership asked everyone in the church to tithe, Stella's heart screamed, *No!* She thought, *I don't even trust you. I feel weird about the decisions you're making. I don't know what to do with this money.*

Stella knew she had to change her thinking and felt that God was showing her His love for her church and her friends there. She knew they couldn't build their church without people like her giving donations regularly, but she still lacked a fundamental trust in the leadership that would make it easier for her tithe.

Then she had a moment of clarity. *You know what?* she thought. *I love God, and I know my treasure is where my heart is, so I'm going to treasure God with my finances. And I treasure other families in my church, so to give financially is right. For some reason I now can feel it's part of how I'm supposed to worship. So I'm going to do that.*

Stella prayed for a number for what to give. She landed on a number well above 10 percent, and it hurt. *I know this is Your nature, God, because it's still hurting mine*, she prayed.

Stella told me, "Even while it hurts, there's a part of you that says, 'Wow, my life is changing now because my value system is tied to God's.'"

That is what tithing and giving money is really about. It is not about God taking your money; it is about your values being aligned to the understanding that all God has is already yours. And if you believe that, giving will not be a struggle.

Sometimes God will ask you to do something you don't think you want to do with your money or resources. For example, "Go buy that family dinner."

You think, *Okay. I know that's God because I wasn't planning on buying anyone dinner. I don't want to buy someone dinner. I like my money.*

Or, "Give that homeless person a ride to the place she needs to go."

You think, *I don't want them to sit in the seat. My seat will stink. I like my Mercedes seats.*

As you move through the struggle, remember that if you follow His lead, He will change you and use your resources for good.

GOD CARES ABOUT FINANCES ON MICRO AND MACRO LEVELS

My friend we'll call Jared is working to bring a reformation to the banking systems, which is the backbone of nations. He learned about the need for a reformation through his intimacy with God. God started to show Jared what the financial world was doing, and He would say, "Contrast that action with how My heart would deal with this situation."

Jared often came back to the truth of Matthew 7:16: "By their fruit you will recognize them." He realized that if you know the fruit, you know the root. If you know the root, you know the DNA. If you know the DNA, you know the source.

That taught Jared how to look at a situation, an establishment, or a system, and then start to discern who the source of the system was. If the system was based on God, he would taste and see that its fruit was love.

God went through a process of showing Jared things in that world that did not have a good source—simple things, such as a mortgage contract, or the laws about loans. And God would ask Jared if he could find Him there, if he could find good fruit in it. Part of the tasting and seeing involved a lengthy legal evaluation of a system's fruit and contrasting it with the fruits of the Spirit. So it was through love and relationship that God helped him identify a system's source by tasting and seeing whether the fruit was good. Jared saw some good fruit and a lot of bad fruit.

He is now spearheading a new initiative called a community bank, which is a not-for-profit bank, and meeting up with others who also have a reformer mind-set toward banking. He has found, however, that it's hard to find people in the church who sense the same calling. Jared told me, "It's true that many of us can see that finance doesn't work for the general good of the general population. It offers a service and a process. It offers a means of exchange and a way to do business. That's about where it stops for the average individual."

People have prophesied over Jared about abolishing debt slavery. He said, "God spoke to me, and I realized I was an abolitionist, believing that slavery is one of the things that holds us back from our true potential in God. Then I applied that to debt and saw debt slavery was holding back whole nations of people."

Jared began to form a new banking system so that every interaction would be weighed against the responsibility of love. "I realized that anything that doesn't have a source in love is not only irrelevant; it's actually death. I know that's a bit serious, but hey, let's get this right. There are only two trees. There's love, and there's fear. Fear is death, and love is life."

One of the main points Jared returns to is that power is money. He shared how God hates the disproportionate distribution of power on earth. That revelation was part of his encounter with God's love on this subject. Jared believes that God is judging the system and that God is saying, "I have something that's better than what is currently in place, and it will show My love nature in the banking area of your lives. There's a better way."

If you talk to anyone who is making a great impact on a social justice issue, bringing a new technology to the world, or developing a medical breakthrough, money and resources were involved in creating the opportunity for it to happen. God wants us to anticipate that there are resources for us to steward.

When you start to see who He loves, you start to see how able He is to resource them with anything it would take to recreate His original version of them. Hearing God causes us to access provision because we've learned that finances are a conduit of love.

11

PROPHECY IN GOVERNMENT

When you read the Bible, you start to see a theme that God is a king and a leader, and He cares about societies and how they are managed. In the beginning He provided humanity with His perfect governmental plan, one that would create a utopia. Even after Adam and Eve left the garden, God showed that He still cared about governments. He formed a nation of His very own people, Israel. There were rules, laws, and covenants, which all reflected His heart. In the past several thousand years, God has spoken into governments through His people. We also see how Jesus Himself carried a government of love, which is still disrupting nations and people groups today.

I love how Isaiah 9:6–7 says, "The government will be on his shoulders. . . . Of the greatness of his government and peace there will be no end." God's love brings justice, order, and wholeness. When Solomon ruled in the wisdom of it, people from all the nations couldn't help but notice his prophetic wisdom. They'd see Solomon handle problems—the same problems they were facing—using God's powerful ways of governing to find resolution and justice. The Queen of Sheba was so taken with Solomon and his wisdom from God that she said, "Because of the LORD's eternal love for Israel, he has made you king to maintain justice and righteousness" (1 Kings 10:9).

When we see through love's eyes, we start to see that God cares about government.

God is present in policies and procedures in governments today. God has called some of you to impact the world for Him by participating in government, similar to how Daniel and Joseph in the Bible had clear governmental calls. Because they were faithful in their roles, their people groups were saved and the kingdoms they served had grace extended to them, even throughout droughts, famines, and wars.

Over the years I've seen many people in politics be open to prophecies, some of which have brought clarity to the most complicated issues. These government officials will have spent so much time struggling to find a solution, working with some of the most educated people in the world, and then a Christian will show up and give a word from God that had never before entered a human mind.

It's amazing that the more we look at the Father, the more we see that our potential for impact is not limited to our own capabilities. We can become more than we thought we could be. Looking at the Father also usually results in getting a revelation for our cities and realizing how much He is already doing. Our focus will shift away from all the fighting about which political parties are right, all the fear and anger. We will instead start to think in terms of God's kingdom and His government. So many things will no longer matter because we can be assured that God is on the throne. We can become obsessed with God, knowing that natural politics are small compared with spiritual politics.

AN ANGEL'S GOVERNMENTAL ASSIGNMENT IN KOREA

I think it's important for Christians to pursue politics and government from God's perspective, but there also are times when God's government pursues us.

One day when I was enjoying some time off at home, playing video games, a man suddenly appeared in my room. No one was supposed to come over. When I looked up I knew he was not a human being. He was bare chested and muscular, with Asian features. I had a strong sense that this was an angel, and I was in shock.

I have the fear of the Lord, and in that moment, I could feel His love for the nation of Korea. (People always ask me, "South or North?" But I couldn't identify it for either one; I could just feel the love of God for Korea.)

The angel said, "We're strong there." He started to lay out what has happened in the last sixty years, showing me that Korea was like a Polaroid picture that got fully developed. It started as a third world nation and changed exponentially. This is what the kingdom can do. Christians went in and replanted the country.

Now it's a leader in scientific technology—computer science, agricultural science, water agricultural science. Korea is excelling at the top of the list in these areas of study and innovation. It is also considered the most Christian nation in Asia now.

If it had not been developed as a nation, what would have happened to our world? Some of the technologies that the world is using, for sustainable food, for example, came from Korea.

Then I started to wonder about other countries, such as Indonesia, Venezuela, and some in Africa. What about these third world nations that have a destiny, God's original intention for them? Surely there are inventions, scientific discoveries, and other types of accomplishments they're destined for. I began to see these nations pregnant with the potential of these great works, but those works were unable to come forth until God made a kingdom investment and reinstitutionalized the culture in these areas.

The Korean angel was still in my room and said, "God is going to bring a bridge. South Korea has gotten off track with the Western world, and God is going to bring a bridge by raising up a president who won't be loved by the church. But he is a Christian and the Lord loves him. I want you to go and help him get elected."

"Okay, sure," I said. I wasn't being sarcastic, as if I didn't believe him, but I just couldn't imagine how I could have any part in this. I honestly didn't even know exactly where Korea was on a map. I couldn't point out this politician if I saw him in a picture. I knew nothing about him.

"Is there a time frame?" I asked.

"Yes, you'll go in April."

Well, it was already March.

"April five years from now?" I replied. "Because I have plans. I have a whole month of trips scheduled for this April. I may have one trip cancel a year, so . . . I can't see how this April will work."

Wow, was I wrong. As it turned out, *all* my trips in April were canceled.

Long story short, I was invited to go to South Korea on a ministry trip. It was my entry trip. Three months later I was invited to come back for a conference, and when I did, a woman came up to me after a meeting the last night I was there. She asked if I would come meet some people at her house. It was very late and stormy, and I was going to say no, but I felt God say, "This is the starting point of the work the angel told you about." So I went.

When I arrived at her house, I met a lot of people who filled me with a vision for the country, and I fell in love with them all. During that time my host told me she knew a man who was running for president and asked if I could come meet with him soon.

The Lord said, "This is your appointment."

During that visit I had already met with four other people who were running for president. I thought, *This is overload.*

But I did agree, and I ended up going to the office of a man who used to be governor and was now running for presidential office. He was clearly exhausted, looking as if he might fall asleep while I was talking to him.

All of a sudden the presence of God came, and He said to me, "This is the man. I want you to pray for him. He needs seven brains."

He needs seven brains?

"Yes. He'll understand it. He needs seven brains to run

the country. He feels that he has only one brain. He needs an expansion of his mind because he doesn't understand enough, but he understands a few things. He knows that there is going to be unification between North and South Korea, and that their relationship with America is an important one." And the Lord continued to speak to me about a number of things this man needed.

Then I told the man some issues he was going to have to be honest about to win the election. It was intense. I spoke as if I had authority over this future president. I prophesied over him, saying the kingdom of heaven had come upon me. I gave him some instructions.

He looked at me and asked, "Am I going to win?"

"If you follow the instructions of the Lord, you'll win," I answered.

At this point he didn't have great popularity. He was visible but not very popular.

I went back six more times that year, making a total of seven trips. I was interviewed by all the megachurches. "What is God's word for South Korea?" they asked me.

I told them that God was about to make South Korea a gateway to Asia on the map, and that God was going to reestablish it in business, government, politics, and the church with all the Western countries it needed connection with. I said that the glory of God was in Korea and was going to raise up North Korea, which had the same technology gift as South Korea did. I said there'd be a cheap labor force, which would establish Korea's economy across the globe as one of the most powerful economies in a short period of time.

I prophesied this all over South Korea, and as I did, people kept asking me about the president. Their version of CNN invited me to do an interview on the national news about how God was going to elect President Lee. I wanted to say, "I was playing a video game. That's it. I was shooting people in a video game. God knows where He can apprehend me."

Later on, two months before this man was elected, I went to South Korea one more time. I did quite a bit of what I call spiritual campaigning for him. Churches responded by saying to me, "We're reassessing our viewpoint on this man." At that point it was down to him and two other people, and he was the only Christian in the running. They said, "We really believe that something shifted, but we don't trust his politics."

"Well, you don't have to trust all of them, but there may be some things that God wants to do through him," I told them. "It's better to have someone who at least has the heart and the ear of God versus somebody who doesn't. You may consider that."

Shortly after I got home from that last trip, I received word that he'd been elected president. I knew it was one step forward in God's plan to show that He loves South Koreans and North Koreans and to unify them.

God also loves the whole world and has put technology and education in Korea that we all need. We have had an installment of it, but He wants to give the world more through Korea. He wants to use both people in government and people outside the government to bring about the changes that need to happen.

But this is not a special situation. All over the world God wants us to care for and love those in government. It is not about choosing a side or political party. It is about loving people in leadership and helping them align with God's heart and vision for a country.

INFLUENCING ECUADORIAN POLICYMAKERS

My friend Jennifer had an incredible experience working with the government when she and her team were ministering in Ecuador.

"Justice is central to the gospel, so to me, it's part of everything we do," said Jennifer. "I believe justice is the restoration of every violation of love. Any situation where God's original dream for an individual or community has been violated, justice can come in and set it right.

"We've been working in Ecuador for a long time with the issue of human trafficking. My team and I began going out on the streets with a simple approach: we loved on people and ministered to them. But the enormity of the problem went beyond our reach. We got to the point where we said, 'We've got to find a way to heal this issue. We're tired of picking up bodies. This country has no legislation that protects victims of trafficking, so we have to go to the root of this problem.'

"We began to pray, *God, will You help us to get inside the government so we can influence this issue?* We asked God for strategy and access, and He gave it to us, because He's good."

It's easy to say, "I'm one person. What can I do?" But the reality is, we can say instead, "I have everything I need because Christ is in me. I have access to everything in the kingdom."

What happened next is that Jennifer assigned a twenty-two-year-old team member we'll call Kendall to this task. She told her, "It's your full-time job to figure out how we get into the government. For a year, that's your job." Kendall began to pray and seek God.

One day Kendall came across a website with contact

information for the three top policymakers in Ecuador. She quickly wrote down the information. When she refreshed the web page, the contact information was gone.

Another team member said, "That was Jesus." The rest of the team agreed.

"What do I do?" Kendall asked.

"You email them. That's what you do," Jennifer told her. "He gave you an email address!"

So Kendall emailed them, saying, "Helping victims of sexual exploitation is our passion. We want to serve you and help you in what you are doing and explore how we might help these victims."

One of the policymakers responded positively.

"I think it was because it was clear our approach was to love and to serve," Jennifer said. "So often Christians tell people what they're doing wrong, and that's not getting anybody anywhere."

The policymaker said in her reply, "This is so interesting. Can I have lunch with you?"

Through that connection Kendall was offered a job as a news anchor at the government-run TV station. Random, right? It's important to notice how one step leads to another, though. Kendall was a good steward there, and she earned the opportunity to run her own show. She conducted interviews and had such powerful conversations that her show became the highest-rated show on TV. Her boss wanted to fire her because she discussed controversial topics, but he couldn't because she had such great ratings.

One day Kendall interviewed an Olympic champion who had lost his legs. Later he told her, "What you don't know about me is that I am the personal trainer of the president. I showed him the interview you did with me, and he said, 'I've never seen a journalist pull light out of somebody like this girl did. I want her to interview me.'"

As you can see, things progressed little by little. But none of these things would have happened unless they'd started out simply loving people on the streets every Thursday night. Then they got to the next step, and then the next. You just have to start somewhere and keep going.

From that day on, Jennifer's team received so much favor with the government that they were given the opportunity to hold a national campaign called Real Men Don't Buy Women. As it aired on national television, they were able to preach to the whole country and call them to end modern-day slavery. It started a national conversation.

Government officials were so intrigued that they sent their top policymakers to Jennifer's team, asking, "Will you help us write the legislation in this country?" And the team helped make important changes to policies that changed people's lives.

I tell you this crazy story because it's honestly that simple. We think (especially as Americans), "Oh, we need the government to fix a problem." No, you don't. You have the kingdom of God. You need connections, and you need money, but God can provide. Whatever is needed for a change—one that is in line with His heart—is available to you.

I am so passionate for the body of Christ to grab hold of this, because it's working. In every country I visit, I meet radical believers who are advancing the kingdom of God. This is who we are, and this is what we get to do. This is the exciting call on our lives!

12

PROPHECY IN
REDEMPTION

There are times when things cannot be restored to us in the way they were lost, and there are some things that are lost forever. We cannot pretend this doesn't happen; it's simply part of life in this world. Some people we will lose forever because they fell away from God. Some broken relationships cannot be restored on earth. Some things have been taken away from us, or we have lost them and will never find them, even if we pray. All of this can leave our hearts weary and disappointed.

But when we turn to God, He will comfort us and help us learn how to respond to disappointments. He gives us hope through His promise in Romans 8:28—that He will use hardships to bring us good.

God is also a Father who disciplines those He loves. That means He guides us in life and makes sure we develop character and substance. Maybe He took away something that was going to destroy us; maybe He was protecting us. Perhaps we'll learn something we never would've learned if we hadn't followed Him down a difficult path to redemption. Or it could be something changed simply because the old had to die so that something better could come to life.

When something like this happens, we should be expectant. For everything that is taken away, God has a plan to redeem it. He'll bring good not just through a replacement but through some kind of upgrade or life-giving process.

REDEMPTION AFTER EARTHQUAKE DESTRUCTION

Back in 1999 I prophesied over a pastor in Peru. Afterward I called him and said, "God has shown me that there's going to be about an 8.0 earthquake in your city. I'm glad to be able to tell you, though, because God is warning you. He is good enough to give you this foreknowledge. Have everyone in your city prepare and get earthquake insurance.

"Ultimately, Lima will benefit from this. You'll be able to create better buildings. If I'm right, you're going to come out of this with a lot of money. If I'm wrong, you'll just have some good prayer meetings. But I sense that it's going to happen this day."

So, my pastor friend, who was connected to the whole city, told business owners, government officials, and church leaders about my word of the coming earthquake as well as predictions from seismologists that seismic activity would occur during the same time frame. He rallied the city to make preparations.

He felt compelled to reach out especially to two bigger churches that he didn't have strong relationships with but that he really loved. He said to them, "Our church is planning to go to a retreat center several hours away. Would you like to join us? We could even have a citywide church retreat—invite all the churches to meet in a big open area and camp out there together. It could be like a Christian Woodstock."

The churches said yes, and about seventeen thousand people ended up leaving the city for a week to pray and hang out with Jesus and worship. During that time there was an earthquake in Lima, and no one was in any of the buildings owned by church members. Everyone who trusted and believed in the word kept people out of their buildings and had earthquake insurance.

There was, of course, a lot of damage. Many of the city's buildings were destroyed. Had God not spoken and had they not purchased insurance, it would have been easy to wonder why God had let it happen. When I went to visit the city two years later, these three churches had seen the redemption of God in the destruction. They'd received millions of dollars to rebuild their city, so there were beautiful new buildings with state-of-the-art construction.

The church had gained more authority because they had become so strong financially (because God had forewarned them), and this was giving them the ability to bring some great changes for the city and region around them as they started to see social projects and development projects they could contribute to. It caused their city to take notice of them; they had not previously known anyone in the government. But now their church was known and a part of many city-led efforts starting to transform the region. Not only that, it brought salvation—thousands of people had been saved and were excited to be living for God.

I saw the power of our God, who wants us to invest in community strategy and give people wisdom to avoid evil. That's our God. The Enemy is under His feet. He's not worried about our sin; He's worried about His inheritance. That's what God's focused on. Sin only blocks His inheritance. "But in these last days he has spoken to us by his Son, whom he appointed heir of all things, and through whom also he made the universe" (Hebrews 1:2).

He removes sin by turning people's hearts to Him. He doesn't remove sin by destroying rebellious people. If He did, corrupt leaders in North Korea would be dissolved right now. If He did, the Nazi movement never would have happened. If He did, there would have been a totally different outcome of World War II. God wants hearts to turn to Him; He doesn't want to destroy people.

REDEMPTION AFTER DIVORCE

My friend ReyShawn saw through the eyes of love to overcome a horrible betrayal, which would have set him back many years if he'd been looking through natural eyes. But looking through God's eyes of love toward himself and his situation, he saw what was possible and experienced tremendous redemption. I have been blessed to be on this journey with him.

On a seemingly normal day, ReyShawn left work to meet his wife, who we'll call Kat, for lunch and came back to work with his life completely changed, ambushed by betrayal.

Kat had been his best friend for years. She'd lived with him, served God with him, and made promises to him. He had been building and investing in his marriage for eight years, and it all came crashing down within about twenty minutes, before they even sat down to their lunch reservation.

The relationship had been going in a difficult direction since Kat had started making hurtful decisions, but ReyShawn had chosen to believe the best. He had been sure that with his love and support, and with God's love and support, their issues would be resolved, their relationship would be restored, and they would come out of the challenges together.

ReyShawn learned that day, however, that Kat had betrayed him in almost every area of life—finances, assets, relationships, family, and emotions. Within a matter of minutes, ReyShawn went from having a stable home to returning to his house only to quickly grab what he could and having to ask friends for a place to stay.

ReyShawn said it was as if he and Kat were driving down the road of life together, heading in a direction they had agreed on. And out of nowhere Kat reached over and ripped out his heart, then jerked the steering wheel, crashing the car and destroying them both.

It affected every area of his life with unbelievable pain.

It is easy at the point of betrayal to question everything you thought you knew about your life and to believe that one betrayal means no one can be trusted. But I watched ReyShawn guard his heart in this situation. He believed in his core that God had never intended this for him.

When someone hurts us, it is important to remember that it is not God's fault. Believing the best protects our hearts and keeps us in a healthy place to see through eyes of love, but it does not guarantee that another person will not hurt us. We don't have control over that, and we never will. Even God doesn't have control over people hurting Him. In fact, He has been hurt by people more than any of us ever will be! People make their own choices, and if those choices separate them from God, from their commitments, and from their relationships, there will always be consequences.

Instead of pushing God's love away, ReyShawn believed God was still on his team and still his number one support. ReyShawn didn't ask God why. To him, that answer was easy. Kat had made choices that devastated and damaged their relationships with God and others. God had simply given all people free will, so ReyShawn refused to blame God. Blaming God would have only caused separation from Him and led to more devastation in his life, mind, body, and heart.

ReyShawn's relationship with God was still his number one relationship. He believed God was his Father and best Friend, and he needed that relationship for strength and comfort in such a hard time. He believed that God turned all things, even the worst things, to good, even when it did not look possible. He believed God was the only solution to his survival and a good future.

My wife, Cherie, was the first person ReyShawn told about this, and I reached out to him as soon as possible. He ended up staying with us for about a month so he would have a safe place to be.

ReyShawn was concerned for Kat as she was bringing so much destruction into her life. He chose to fulfill his promise to care for her by paying rent and financially providing for her, even though she had broken every promise to him. ReyShawn believed his promise was primarily to God, not to her, and God would reward and honor that decision, even if she never did. He had committed himself to God even more than he had to her, so he wouldn't let her actions cause him to break his promise to God.

ReyShawn realized that keeping his heart pure was his responsibility; it didn't depend on the actions of others. He followed Jesus' model and started to pray for Kat every time she came to mind. Instead of focusing on his hurt and what she did to him, he focused on interceding for her. He asked God to get in the way of the destruction she was bringing into her own life and to also bring others into Kat's life to show love to her. ReyShawn said this prayer was like medicine and helped him heal. I think that's because he remained committed to seeing everything through the eyes of love.

It was beautiful to see how God was with ReyShawn during that time. God immediately sent wonderful friends to help him deal with the shock and to stop the emotional bleeding from the metaphorical car crash. God sent people who offered tangible expressions of His love and care to him.

Sometimes God speaks love through others, as He did with ReyShawn at that point. Other times He speaks love directly to us. God speaks words that heal, soothe, comfort, and empower us in ways that the words of others never could. This is what happened next for ReyShawn.

A few weeks after the lunch meeting, ReyShawn was driving to work and asking God to help him understand his situation and heal his heart. He invited God to share His thoughts about what had happened. Immediately, ReyShawn heard God's voice inside his mind.

"Do you want to know how I relate to your story?"

Yes!

Then God named a date. It was a date in the past, several months before the betrayal. He said, "This was the day she betrayed Me."

God told ReyShawn the situation and shared details, and said Kat had broken His heart. He told ReyShawn about the pain He'd felt going through it Himself. He showed ReyShawn where His love for him was in every moment of his pain. God showed him what He was doing to help him, how He'd protected him as much as possible, and how at that very moment He was caring for his heart. God promised He had good things in mind for redemption in the future.

ReyShawn said this brought him to a deep, intimate place with God. He was able to share with God the pain they both had experienced, and he knew God understood him perfectly.

God then showed ReyShawn Jesus' heart in the moments when He Himself had been betrayed and how hard it had been. (Jesus knows betrayal better than any of us!) ReyShawn realized that God could relate and was certainly qualified to help him.

In that encounter in the car, God brought ReyShawn through the most beautiful inner healing. ReyShawn came to know that above everything else, he was loved. The cavity of pain in his heart became like a deep well filling up with the love of God. And he could see that God's love was powerful enough to make everything turn out not just okay but even better than before. He now was able to dream again and believe in good things for his life. He felt as if he got his life back.

In the months that followed, ReyShawn realized that aligning himself with God's love meant aligning with enduring strength, greater love, and ultimate victory. He was partaking in the victory that Jesus had after He had been betrayed and had risen from the dead. The parts of him that died in that relational car crash were also raised from the dead with Christ, and because he did not disconnect from God, he began to live a more abundant life.

I have never seen anyone go through what ReyShawn went through with such dignity and emotional stability. His focus on God's love for him helped him thrive, when others in his same situation may never have recovered or may have taken twenty years or more to recover.

What God did for Job He did—and is still doing—for ReyShawn. What was stolen became a seed that, when watered in love, became even greater and more abundant! Every area of his life that was hurt, taken, and damaged was redeemed, and he has begun to receive a double or triple portion of what he lost, if not more. Relationally, spiritually, emotionally, and financially, he has begun to see an incredible harvest of good fruit in his life.

God truly is a God of redemption, and the only way we can experience that redemption is through Him. ReyShawn's story is a reminder that nothing that is lost or taken can prevent us from receiving God's love, which can transform our loss to increased gain.

THERE IS NOTHING GOD CAN'T REDEEM

God can bring redemption to all areas of life, including our work and ministry.

My friend we'll call Sam was in a really good place in life when he prayed, *God, burn up everything in me that's not*

Jesus—and use the blowtorch. He jokes that God enlisted the Devil to do the work. I think Sam made a good point, though; sometimes the Devil will bring something threatening, like a blowtorch, with the intent to hurt us, but it ends up killing parts of ourselves we want to get rid of and surrender to God anyway. Sometimes God allows us to lose things so He can connect us to something better—something we never would have reached if the loss hadn't motivated us toward change.

Sam and his wife, Lucy, were really blessed to get involved with an amazing church and movement and were brought into leadership. They planted churches, pioneered mission schools, and served as copastors. Then there were some changes. One of their best friends stepped into leadership, and he felt insecure and threatened by having his friends continue to lead because he knew they were further along in life with grown kids and grandkids as well as endeared by the church around them; this made him feel insecure. So, they were demoted from leading programs they had started. They ended up leaving the church, and it was a really painful time. It was hard to understand and seemed unjust.

Had the pain not come, they probably never would have left that church. The pain motivated them to change and think of other options for their lives. That didn't come easily because they were loyal people. They had years of blessing, and then there was a year of meltdown when nothing seemed to be working well.

Someone prophesied over them, saying, "Run for your life."

Another prophet said, "This is like Joseph and his brethren. You need to flee."

Yet they weren't sure where to go at the time. The only leading they felt they might have received from God was about pastoring a church on the other side of the country, one that it seemed no one else wanted to pastor.

One day Sam asked Lucy, "Why don't you pray about this specifically right now, because I think I heard something."

Lucy prayed, "God, I'm in so much pain. I don't know if I trust myself. If You want us to move, let our house sell for full price the first day it's on the market to the first person who walks in, and let that person pay cash."

Sam thought it would never happen. He thought maybe it'd be best to quit ministry, go build houses, and give lots of offerings to poor, suffering pastors.

They listed the house the next morning, and by eleven o'clock that same morning, they were told, "A man wants to come see your house."

The man came and by the time he left, there was an offer on the table for the full price in cash.

So ten days later they packed up a U-Haul truck and headed across the country, wondering if they were crazy and if they were destroying their lives. When they arrived, it was bleak and disappointing. The little church group had recommended a townhouse for them, and they'd signed a lease without seeing it. They had both grown up and lived in beautiful places, and to them the property was very ugly. Their view was of an Exxon oil tank farm next to a railroad track.

They could have given up right then and there, but instead, they thought of God's process. They knew they were not carrying out their own process or plan. They were leaning into God, saying, *We'll follow You.*

I think a lot of people get stuck in the middle of the struggle; they just cannot come out of a situation like that because they don't take God on the journey with them. A lot of people would probably just do whatever they could in their own strength to fix the situation.

But Sam and Lucy stayed there with the attitude of, *We're in Your hands, God.*

During that time He healed their hearts in a beautiful way that can only happen when you're not in intense activity. When you're thriving and succeeding in a lot of things, you can hide bitterness and resentment so easily. It was an intense time with God pruning a bunch of stuff out of them and reshaping them.

For the first six months, Sam and Lucy had no idea what they were doing there, and it felt like a punishment. The church they were serving was dysfunctional, and they would cry out, *God, what was our crime that led to this? What did we do? Why are You doing this to us?* As they kept praying and crying out, God continued to heal them of many things. They also forgave people for the injustice of the situation at their old church.

Sam and Lucy ended up attending some services at another church nearby, and the pastor there asked them, "What are you doing here?"

"Well, we came to lead this little church," Sam answered.

"You know," said the pastor, "sometimes you come to a place and you think you're there for one reason, but you're actually there for something else."

Sam and Lucy honestly hoped that was true in their case. They were thinking, *We've been downgraded. We went from this amazing church with a reputation for the presence of God to a church with eight people who are really grouchy. Not exactly good team members for church planting!*

Eventually the small church closed down, and the pastor

they'd met at the other church nearby invited Sam to preach. Sam was so full of joy because he really valued the opportunity to get to preach at a large church again. He felt alive. Then the pastor told Sam that he had received a prophetic word that someone like Sam would come to their church.

Nine months after Sam and Lucy moved they were offered positions at this other church, which was eventually launched into renewal and revival. The calling God had for them was redeemed as they stepped into something even greater for their lives!

Within a couple of years Sam and Lucy had restored their relationships with the leaders at their old church. When the pastor there was nearing his death, he said he wanted them to come back and lead the church. They couldn't because they were already in the middle of a big miracle in their new church, and they knew they were meant to be there. When the pastor of their old church died, God used Sam and Lucy to find a replacement pastor for their old church. And in the early days of the renewal, when they were traveling, other leaders from their old church traveled with them. The relationships were restored, and their positions were redeemed and upgraded. There was a happy ending for them all.

The great truth I like to come back to when I think about this story is that God loves *everyone*. Sam and Lucy talk about it with this reminder: "Even if someone treats you badly, or you think they treated you badly, God's not going to kill them. He's going to make them better."

When intimacy with God is your goal in life, you begin to see hardships differently. You expect to hear God and see His redemption. It's not that you're wearing rose-colored glasses; you actually have a truer perspective. You see through His eyes. And you have unique expectations and outcomes.

When redemption is needed in a relationship, your heart isn't saying, "Fix this. Get them to repent to me." It's not about that anymore. It's not about you. It's about what's at stake in the big picture, about God making broken things whole and beautiful. That was Jesus' attitude as He went to the cross.

God wants us to live with a full measure of love. We have to choose to see things through His lens, to see that everything can be restored or redeemed.

Whenever you are struggling with this, you have a Counselor, the Holy Spirit, who can come to you like a life coach. Ask Him to help you reset what you believe about the pain you have had in your life and walk in a new direction of healing and redemption.

CONCLUSION

THE WORLD NEEDS YOU

Some of you are highly educated, but not all of you are. I'm not. I am life educated, and I've taught at Bible school since I was nineteen.

A few years ago I taught 750 PhD students in Asia. My hosts knew that if they told the students right away that I didn't have a PhD, they'd be setting me up for failure; the students immediately would not listen.

I was looking at them through God's eyes, so I felt no intimidation, just love.

We ended up having an incredible teaching time. God came to us in a powerful way that touched everyone. At the end of our session, my hosts told the crowd of students, "Just so you know, Shawn doesn't have a college education."

Everyone was shocked.

"That's what the prophetic does!" I said.

I value formal education, and sometimes that's what God uses to impart His wisdom to people. But there are many other types of wisdom His people can excel in. The prophetic upgrades you. It upgrades you to opportunities that you would never get based on your own credentials or abilities. The prophetic can bypass your education or socioeconomic status, because wisdom comes from God. As I said in earlier in this book, love needs no qualifications or degrees to empower it to be effective.

The world is looking for people who have unnatural authority (the world has seen what natural authority does). They want people who are filled with God. They're looking for people who can change policies, who can change cultural mind-sets, who can change their lives for the better. As Christians, we're the ones who are standing in between heaven and earth. We're the only ones who can get consistently good, bright ideas.

Whatever happens on your prophetic journey, it's important that you keep your heart as open as possible to hearing God. Take risks. Believe that God is able to lead you and show you His heart.

You will master risk-taking in the prophetic only after you've done it over and over—thousands of times. Don't get discouraged early on, because you're going to learn so much through your experiences if you don't give up. It's not about being right your first thousand times; it's about learning who God is, learning who you are, and learning how to see through the eyes of love.

What would happen if love was our lens, and we could actually perceive what was in God's deepest thoughts for the world, for our families and friends, for ourselves? Hopefully the stories and discussions in this book have expanded your expectations. Anything is possible with God. I am constantly amazed at His love nature. He does whatever it takes to love people.

And you are someone He loves!

Now let's look through those eyes of love and help the world become the place God originally dreamed of. Let's bring words that restore, redeem, and connect His amazing power and heart to people's lives!

ACKNOWLEDGMENTS

I want to thank my team, my family, for being the greatest catalyst for love. I see through their eyes and I see Jesus. My wife, daughters, parents, siblings—I am so grateful.

I also want to thank Jeremy and Ally Butrous for helping to put this together and sharing some of their stories within the pages. Thank you for working with me to bring love onto paper for others to have a fresh glimpse of what love can look like. Thanks as well to our Bolz Ministries team.

I also want to thank all those who have helped me love well and all those who have let me love them. I have learned so much from love and am so glad that it is the substance of God's nature.

I lastly want to thank whoever designed emojis so my daughters can express the fullness of their love through the kitty heart eyes emoji as well as all other girly emojis that bring us all so much joy.

ABOUT THE AUTHOR

Shawn Bolz is an author, host of a popular podcast called *Exploring the Prophetic*, a TV host spiritual adviser, and a minister. He is passionate about seeing individuals and groups learn how to be the most connected, best version of themselves through their relationships with God.

Shawn has been a pioneer in ministry, including the prophetic movement, since he was in his teens. His focus on a genuine relationship with God, creativity through entertainment, and social justice has brought him around the world to meet with churches, CEOs, entertainers, and world leaders.

Shawn is the founding pastor of Expression58 Christian Ministries, a ministry focused on the entertainment industry and the poor in Los Angeles, California, where he lives with his wife, Cherie, and their two daughters. He can often be found trying out new coffee places or playing video games.

Check out this resource and
many others by Shawn Bolz at
BolzMinistries.com

BREAKTHROUGH:
PROPHECIES, PRAYERS,
AND DECLARATIONS

MINISTRIES